# authentic relationships

**Other Books by Wayne Jacobsen**

*He Loves Me!*
*In My Father's Vineyard*
*The Naked Church*
*Tales of the Vine*
*Pathways of Grace*

**Other Books by Clay Jacobsen**

*Interview with the Devil*
*Circle of Seven*
*The Lasko Interview*

# authentic relationships

## discover the lost art of "one anothering"

WAYNE JACOBSEN & CLAY JACOBSEN

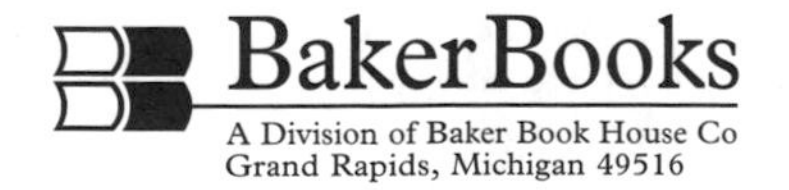
BakerBooks
A Division of Baker Book House Co
Grand Rapids, Michigan 49516

Published by Baker Books
a division of Baker Publishing Group
P.O. Box 6287, Grand Rapids, MI 49516-6287
www.bakerbooks.com

Printed in the United States of America



Library of Congress Cataloging-in-Publication Data

Jacobsen, Wayne
Authentic relationships : discover the lost art of "one anothering" / Wayne Jacobsen and Clay Jacobsen.
p. cm.
Includes bibliographical references and index.
ISBN 10: 0-8010-6451-1 (pbk.)
ISBN 978-0-8010-6451-7 (pbk.)
1. Fellowship—Religious aspects—Christianity. I. Jacobsen, Clay, 1956- II. Title.
BV4517.5.J33 2003
241′.677—dc21 2003009297



12 13 14 15 16 12 11 10 9 8 7

# contents

# dedications

My wife and I were in Australia four years ago when our good friend Ben Tarren brought up the idea of writing a study guide on the concepts of one anothering that I had woven throughout my first novel. His suggestion led to my participation in the book you now hold in your hands. I gratefully thank you, Ben, for planting the seed.

And to Cindy, my wife and my deepest one anothering partner on this journey—I thank you for helping me with the writing and for sharing your passion about these principles. I'm grateful for your pushing me to see Ben's idea finally come to fruition.

Clay

To the past and present board members at Lifestream who have one anothered Sara and me through the best and worst of times, I thank you for your words of encouragement, wise counsel, prayers, personal support, and rich friendship: Rich and Sheila Artis, Ron and Jen Brisco, Paul and Louise Gutierrez, Jim and Margaret Oliveras, Nelson and Shannon Schwamb, Nick and Julia Sembrano, and Phil and Sheri Shannon.

Wayne

We also want to express our thanks to Vicki Crumpton and all the incredible staff at Baker Books who made this project a better book than we ever could have produced on our own.

Wayne & Clay

We have found that cowritten books can often be disruptive for the reader when the authors try to identify who made what contributions. Wanting to avoid that here, we have chosen to present the material seamlessly as if the words flowed from the mind of only one author. Suffice it to say that this work represents the combination of our passion, wisdom, and experiences, and the "I" in this book may refer to Wayne or Clay or to our combined work. We did not think it important to make that distinction throughout and by not doing so hoped to model the one anothering we wanted to share with you. Also, we have on occasion changed the names of people in our illustrations to protect their identities whenever confidentiality was warranted, but they are nonetheless true stories of the simple power and joy of one anothering.

# preface

I gazed out the window at the snow-covered hills that surrounded the New England retreat. I had accompanied my brother to the retreat to help lead worship. I was not prepared for the revelation the Holy Spirit would birth in my heart that day. Wayne was speaking on the power of Christian friendship, focusing on Scriptures he called the "one anothering" passages.

At first blush his message didn't seem to be anything new. I had been raised by loving, Christian parents and had read these verses individually dozens of times. Though many of them were some of the most endearing passages I had studied in the course of my life, I had never considered them together in this context. Combined, they painted a rich panorama of the incredible relationships of love and support the body of Christ can share.

My retreat experience was a powerful, life-changing moment in my walk with the Lord. As I began to grasp the lost art of one anothering, I started on a journey that has redefined how I view the church, how I relate to other Christians, and even how I relate to God. It also has helped me cultivate better friendships with other believers and people in the world who do not yet know God.

Now, ten years later, my brother and I have walked different paths, but God has brought us together to explore this concept with you. We will investigate such questions as, How can we share meaningful and supportive relationships with other believers? and What is the New Testament model for loving, nurturing friendships? If you have ever hungered for deeper relationships with other believers, perhaps you are ready to realize the difference between going to church and being the church.

Just look at all the ways we can share relationships with other believers:

## One Anothering

**Loving** one another (John 13:34)
**Forgiving** one another (Ephesians 4:32)
**Accepting** one another (Romans 15:7)
**Bearing with** one another (Ephesians 4:2)
**Being devoted to** one another (Romans 12:10)
**Honoring** one another above ourselves (Romans 12:10)
**Greeting** one another (2 Corinthians 13:12)
**Being hospitable to** one another (1 Peter 4:9)
**Being kind and compassionate to** one another (Ephesians 4:32)
**Sharing with** one another (Hebrews 13:16)
**Serving** one another (Galatians 5:13)
**Carrying** one another's **burdens** (Galatians 6:2)
**Building up** one another (1 Thessalonians 5:11)
**Encouraging** one another daily (Hebrews 3:13)
**Comforting** one another (1 Thessalonians 4:18)
**Stimulating** one another **to love and good deeds** (Hebrews 10:24)

**Instructing** one another (Romans 15:14)
**Admonishing** one another (Colossians 3:16)
**Praying for** one another (James 5:16)
**Confessing your sins to** one another (James 5:16)
**Being of the same mind toward** one another (Romans 12:16)
**Submitting to** one another (Ephesians 5:21)

Discovering the significance of these Scriptures has been incredible for me. I pray that your journey with us through this book will help you discover the lost art of one anothering in your own relationships—that is, loving others as God has loved you.

Clay Jacobsen
Camarillo, California

# anyway

People are unreasonable, illogical, and self-centered.
Love them anyway.

If you are kind, people may accuse you of selfish ulterior motives.
Be kind anyway.

If you are successful, you will win some false friends and true enemies.
Succeed anyway.

The good you do today will be forgotten tomorrow.
Be good anyway.

Honesty and frankness will make you vulnerable.
Be honest and frank anyway.

What you spend years building may be destroyed overnight.
Build anyway.

People need help but may attack you if you try to help them.
Help them anyway.

In the final analysis, it is between you and God.
It was never between you and them anyway.

From a sign on the wall of Shishu Bhavan,
a children's home in Calcutta

# 1

# escaping the loneliness trap

People are longing to rediscover true community. We have had enough of loneliness, independence and competition.

Jean Vanier

Anna had never felt so alone. Her husband, Herman, needed minor surgery to repair a hernia, but the fact that he also suffered from Alzheimer's made it anything but minor. The doctor had just visited Herman's room and informed her that after surgery they would have to put her husband in arm and leg restraints. They were concerned he would wake up disoriented and pull out his IV or harm himself in some other way. They didn't have enough staff to keep someone at his bedside throughout recovery.

Anna tried to envision the restraints that would hold her husband immobile. She knew the insurance wouldn't pay for a private nurse, and given his condition he might not even remember it, but the image tormented her nonetheless. What could she do?

A few moments later Anna turned when she heard a knock at the door of her husband's hospital room. Mike and Carol were thirty years younger, but in the last few years they had become good friends through their involvement in the same home fellowship group. Carol noticed the stress in Anna's eyes and was finally able to draw out the cause for her concern. "I know it's probably stupid, but I just don't want him to go through that."

Mike and Carol had no idea what could be done either, but they were on their way to meet with the group and promised Anna they would share her concern and pray about it.

Almost an hour later the phone rang, and Anna grabbed for it before it could awaken her husband.

"Oh good, you're still there." It was Carol.

"After we prayed for you tonight, someone asked why they couldn't just have the nurses keep an eye on Herman. When I explained that the hospital didn't have the staff to do that, she asked if we could do it. Everyone thought that was a great idea, and people started volunteering to take time slots. Anna, would Herman have to be restrained if we had someone in the room with him every moment during recovery?"

"I can't ask you people to do that," Anna said, overwhelmed by the offer.

"You haven't asked—we're offering. Can you find out?"

Anna put down the phone and walked out to the nurses' station. When she returned she told Carol that as long as someone who was awake and alert was with Herman, he wouldn't need to be restrained. Before she could add, "But I don't want you to go to all that trouble," she heard Carol relay the information to the group. The cheers in the background were all she needed to hear.

That night more than a dozen people volunteered for around-the-clock shifts at Herman's bedside while he recovered. When family members heard what Herman and Anna's friends were doing, they volunteered for shifts as well. For the next three days someone was at Herman's side the entire time. As a side benefit Anna had constant companionship through her long hours at the hospital.

A few weeks later Anna tried to thank the group for their incredible demonstration of kindness. Every time she began to speak she was freshly overcome with gratitude. Though everyone in the room appreciated how deeply it had touched her, no one felt like it had been a great sacrifice. They simply had wanted to help a friend through a tough spot.

That group had discovered the simple power of one anothering.

## Isolation in the Communication Age

With our ease of transportation, deluge of cell phones and pagers, and unlimited reach of the Internet, we have more ways to connect with people than ever before. So isn't it ironic that people feel more isolated today?

We work alongside people we don't enjoy, live next door to others we don't know, and even gather in worship services where many feel like just another face in the crowd. Even with close friends many of us can't seem to steer the conversation beyond our children, jobs, weather, or sports to share the depth of our spiritual lives. And when we hurt the most it seems like everyone scatters into the busyness of their own lives.

Anna's story ranks as one of the best examples of friendship among a group of believers that I have ever witnessed.

Unfortunately, this is a great story in part because it is so unique. I could tell far more stories of people going through desperate moments with no one to extend the love and care they needed most. Sometimes it is hard enough to find people who will help you move on a Saturday, much less sit overnight in a hospital with a man who wouldn't recognize them or remember what they had done.

Wittingly or unwittingly, many of us protect ourselves from the kind of friendships that connect us deeply with others. We learned in grade school how fickle relationships can be. Classmates would pretend to be our friend one minute and turn on us the next whenever it would help them get into the "in group" or climb higher in it. Any weakness or dissimilarity became fodder for teasing.

Though the pain of gossip and betrayal becomes subtler in adulthood, it can be just as destructive, if not more so. You would think that our congregations would provide a safe haven from this pain, but too often the opposite is true. "I've never had people in the world treat me as badly as I've been treated by Christians" is a lament I've heard far too often.

Surprisingly, a Sunday morning service can be one of the loneliest places on earth. Who hasn't tried to build new friendships, only to be frustrated by the inability to find one's way into an existing clique? We offer to help others when they are in need, then feel exploited when they are unavailable to help us. Add to that our misplaced expectations, and it is no wonder that many regard relationships as liabilities rather than treasures.

We end up conflicted. Even though we want close relationships, we subvert the desire by holding people at arm's length. Poised to protect ourselves from hurt and disappointment, we think the best solution is to look out for ourselves. There is no better strategy than this for ending up alone and isolated while comfortably blaming others in the process.

Healthy relationships, however, are not created by sitting together in the same building or participating in the same activities, but by capturing Jesus' heart for life-changing relationships. Throughout Jesus' ministry he demonstrated that the simplest acts of love and friendship could reach the most hardened souls and transform them.

## The Lunch That Rocked Zacchaeus's World

Zacchaeus was hoping for a brief glimpse of Jesus, but as it turned out he was not alone. Arriving at the center of town, he could see the street was already lined with people as far as the eye could see. It seemed everyone wanted to see the man from Galilee about whom so many rumors had been spread. Had he really healed the sick and made dead people live again? Could this be the Messiah?

Zacchaeus finally scaled a tree to gain a vantage point. Moments later the Miracle Worker approached. Imagine how fortunate Zacchaeus must have felt when Jesus started to come closer to that tree; and then imagine his utter shock as Jesus paused beneath the tree, told Zacchaeus to come down, and invited himself to Zacchaeus's house for lunch.

The offer itself scandalized the crowd. People turned to one another wondering why Jesus would choose to spend time with someone so despicable. Didn't Zacchaeus consort with Romans to take taxes from his Jewish brothers and sisters? Certainly anyone else in the crowd would have been worthier to spend an afternoon with the Teacher from Galilee.

Zacchaeus knew they were right. Jesus risked ruining his own reputation by befriending him. Yet amazingly Jesus didn't seem to consider it a problem. Zacchaeus had met someone who was truly focused on others—someone who took an interest in him without trying to manipulate him for his own purpose.

Zacchaeus had never seen anyone act that way before. The Romans used him to do their dirty work, and his own countrymen loathed him for it. He had learned long ago that to succeed in life he had to take care of himself even at the expense of others. But this approach to life had left him a lonely man. Jesus penetrated his loneliness with a simple invitation to lunch.

That was the only miracle Zacchaeus needed. As far as we know, he didn't see any blind eyes opened or any lepers healed that day. The simple acts of one anothering—an offer of lunch, an opportunity for a new friendship, and a few hours of conversation—rocked his entire world.

How shallow Zacchaeus's selfishness had to look in the presence of someone who had his eyes focused only on others. Before Jesus moved on, Zacchaeus had promised to give half his possessions to the poor and pay back everyone he had cheated at 400 percent interest.

Every encounter Jesus had was like that. He did not engage people for what he could get out of them, but for what he could give them of God's life. Because he was not focused on himself, he was able to touch people with the deepest treasures of God's love. And that made all the difference.

## Jesus-Centered Friendships

Unfortunately, most of us, like Zacchaeus, are more familiar with the other kind of relationships—people who say they love you but only so long as you benefit them. Because their relationship with you is based on their needs, they can be warm one moment and cold the next.

A friend of mine defines typical relationships as the "mutual accommodation of self-need." He doesn't intend it to be flattering. What he means is that our friendships last only as long as we can satisfy some deep need in each other for security, acceptance, or status. That is why most friendships with other believers are task-oriented and survive only as long as we work on the same task together. As long as you go along with the program, you will find acceptance. However, if you ask the wrong question, miss a few meetings, or even (God forbid!) leave to attend another fellowship, the friendships suddenly stop or turn hostile.

Despite such painful experiences, I am continually amazed at the resiliency of our thirst for genuine friendships. Often we bury it with our busyness, but in the moments when our life slows to a crawl, the craving for friendship emerges. Even people who have been betrayed by those closest to them and have withdrawn from others in a desperate attempt to escape the pain will find themselves in time thirsting again for deep friendships.

We may only experience our desire for friendship as an overwhelming feeling of loneliness, but the reason we have it is because we somehow intuitively know we were created for relationships. It is as if God has wired into our very nature the desire to be connected to his family, so we keep searching for fulfillment even beyond our bitter disappointments. We want people with whom we can share the joys and hurts of our journey and pool our wisdom and resources. We really don't want to make it on our own.

Everywhere I travel I see that thirst throughout the body of Christ, and it often goes unquenched. People have many acquaintances yet few real friendships. We don't know how to make them, cultivate them, or enjoy them and often end up doing the best we can on our own. We can escape this trap only by living the way Jesus did, not trying to get love for ourselves, but learning how to share it with others.

## One Anothering

Whenever I read through the Gospels I am amazed at how little Jesus said about the church. Only Matthew records him using the word and then only twice. Why didn't he tell his followers more about how to organize a church, run its ministries, and plan its services?

I think I know why. He didn't talk about it because he was too busy living it. He became a friend to Zacchaeus, James, John, Peter, Mary, Martha, Lazarus, Nicodemus, a rejected woman at a well who remained nameless, and countless others who came into his proximity. Look at the ways he engaged them, built relationships with them centered in the Father's love, and served them with no thought for himself. That was the power of his kingdom and the secret to living in the joy of his family. With the simple declaration, "I no longer call you servants. . . . I have called you friends" (John 15:15), Jesus identified the nature of the relationship God has always desired with those he created—intimate friendship.

So when Jesus walked among people as the only one who could truly treat others selflessly, the whole world was turned upside down. At the end of his ministry, all he needed to do was tell his followers to go and treat others the same way he had treated them. They knew exactly what he was talking about because they had watched him. We see the marvelous fruit of that in the earliest stages of the life of the church. Jesus' followers were not focused on liturgy, tradition, or growth strategies, but on the power of simple God-centered friendships, both with believers and with those still trapped in the world.

The early believers didn't see themselves as an institution; they saw themselves as a family. Church wasn't something they went to; it was a way of living in relationship with the Father and his other children. Indeed, having learned to love one another, they were unable to restrain themselves from treating others in the world with that same love. It marked them exactly as Jesus said it would—as children of God in a hostile world.

The world marveled at the early church's ability to live selflessly. They had become others-focused like Jesus, and the world was transformed by it. When the apostles summed up the early believers' lifestyle in their letters, they didn't mention much about their organization or their meetings. Instead, they wrote about their relationships and the joy of treating one another the way God had treated them.

Sown throughout the New Testament are the one anothering Scriptures that defined their life together. Many of these are repeated multiple times, but there are twenty-two unique references to their shared life using the words "one another" or "each other." Through the course of these pages, we will examine each of these specific references and see the incredible joy and freedom that results from recovering the lost art of one anothering.

## A Life Focused on Others

If you have ever shared friendships with others-focused people, you know what a treasure those friends are. They take an interest in you just because they care. Their concern is not tied to their own needs and desires in the relationship. Their care for you demands nothing in return and rejoices just to see you blessed. They open their life like a book and let you read it freely. You don't ever have to guess what they are thinking, because they will come right out and tell you, and they make you feel safe enough so that you don't have to pretend with them. They offer their counsel freely but never demand that you follow it. They give you the freedom to disagree and the flexibility to do things differently from how they would do it without ever compromising their love for you.

Almost without thinking they would give you the shirt off their back if they knew you needed it, but they won't always give you everything you want. They look past your faults and celebrate your promise and offer their help to get you there. You may not see them for months or years at a time, but the next time your paths cross, you will feel as though you have never been apart. When they say they will pray for you, you know they will. When you go through your darkest moments, they will stay by your side. They will let their presence comfort you even when the right words escape them.

Such friends find their origin in God's heart. No one can love so freely whom God has not first loved deeply. Discover the power of his love, and you will never be lonely again.

## Discussion Questions

1. Think of one of the most significant relationships you have had in your life other than immediate family. Share about that person briefly and tell what made that relationship so special.
2. Think of one incident in that relationship that illustrates what you valued most about that person. What about friendship did you learn from that incident?
3. Make a list from these stories that defines what your group has already learned about the attributes of friendship.
4. How does this list reflect the ways God has expressed his love to you? Which of these would you like to see in your relationships with other believers as well?

*For guidelines on how to facilitate a small group study, see the appendix on page 151.*

# Part 1

## starting inside

You cannot hope to give to others what you have not received from God himself. One anothering begins on the inside.

# 2

# loving others like god loves you

**"A new command I give you: Love one another. As I have loved you, so you must love one another."**

*John 13:34*

To love another person is to see the face of God.

Les Misérables

I was en route from my home in California to a speaking engagement in Columbus, Ohio, and my flight arrangements had left me with a three-hour layover in Chicago's O'Hare Airport. After finding something to eat, I still arrived at my gate more than two hours before my departure. I sat down to read a book that I wanted to finish before my plane boarded. I had barely settled down to read when the noise of a gathering crowd distracted me. This was before the post–September 11 security measures, and friends and family could greet arriving passengers at the gates.

*Why can't they be quieter?* I asked myself, foolishly expecting the busy concourse to be like a library. The commotion continued to grow until I found it impossible to concentrate. I looked up in contempt as I prepared to move my things to a quieter gate, and a little girl, no older than five, caught my eye. She gazed longingly out the window and then looked up briefly at her mom and smiled as their eyes met.

A burst of laughter pulled my eyes to a young Japanese family, and behind them a young man stood quietly with a single rose in hand. I found myself captured in the human dramas unfolding around me. Their excitement continued to rise until a jet taxied around the terminal and docked at the gate. In the moments until the passengers finally began deplaning, the crowd grew quieter. It would have been easier to read now, but I had forgotten about my book.

Soon people began to come through the jetway. The little girl being held by her mother above the crowd suddenly screamed, "Daddy!" as a man in military uniform came through the door. As her mom put her down, she barged through the crowd and into his arms. The mother joined them in an embrace, nearly crushing the little girl between them. Tears pooled in my eyes.

The Japanese family began to shout greetings in their native language as an elderly couple emerged from the jetway. I wondered if they were the parents of recent immigrants, finally able to see their children's new homeland. Their joy, expressed in tears, deeply hit me, and I tucked my head lest anyone see mine.

I looked at the young man with the rose. He stared intently up the jetway, and with each passenger emerging his face grew more concerned. When the trickle of people finally stopped, his tension was visible. Had she missed her flight? "Oh no, let her be there," I muttered half in prayer. Seconds later she walked out, and his face lit up. He ran to her, and the two lovers embraced.

Soon the crowd, more exuberant than ever, moved up the concourse toward the main terminal. I watched them go with a smile on my face. In just a few moments, my contempt for the annoying crowd had been transformed into deep affection. How it happened reveals one of the most powerful characteristics of God's love.

## One at a Time

I had ceased to view the crowd as a faceless mass of humanity and instead saw them as individuals with unfolding stories. That is how Jesus loved. He did not come to love the Jewish nation or the Roman Empire. He loved those he met in Nazareth, Galilee, Samaria, Jerusalem, and many other places with names long forgotten. He loved in the singular, and as he engaged the lives of the individuals he met, he demonstrated his love for us all.

The first of our one anothering verses comes from Jesus himself in the form of a command: "Love one another. As I have loved you, so you must love one another." He didn't tell his followers to love everyone, but simply the people God put before them. As we have seen, that is how Jesus loved. That kind of love doesn't work en masse; it can only be applied one individual at a time. All the Scriptures we will look at in this study talk about how we treat *one* another. They don't tell us to encourage everyone, serve everyone, admonish everyone, or share with everyone. That would be overwhelming. We sometimes hear, "There's no way I could do that for everyone." We don't have to.

Instead, Jesus frees us to demonstrate love in the moment for whoever is before us. We will never learn to love others if we don't do it one at a time. To help an individual, we don't have to start a ministry and look for others with the same

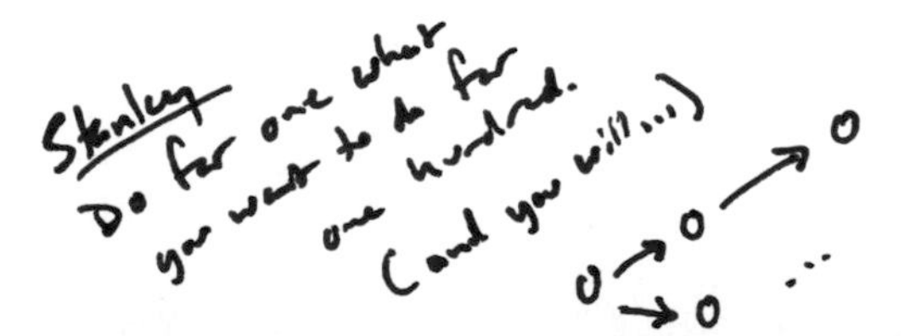

need. Wouldn't it be much better to take the circumstances at hand and do what we can for that person?

I'm reminded of the familiar story of the old scientist lamenting a large group of starfish that had beached themselves at high tide. Shocked by the immense need, he stood paralyzed on the beach until he noticed a little boy grabbing starfish and throwing them back into the ocean.

Spying the old man, the boy rushed over and pleaded, "Mister, you have to help me. We've got to get these starfish back in the ocean before they die." The boy bent over to pick up another one and tossed it back into the waves.

"Do you see how many there are out here?" the scientist asked scanning the shoreline. "What difference can we make?"

The little boy looked down at the starfish he held in his hand, thought a moment, and finally said, "It makes a difference to this one." Then he threw it into the ocean and reached down for another.

## Not Getting but Giving

Whenever I talk about the power of one anothering, many people respond with how great it would be to have friends like that. Usually their next question is, "Where can I find these people?"

Please notice, however, that Jesus didn't say to "get love from each other." He told them simply to love one another. Whenever we focus on what others can do for us instead of what God might ask us to do for them, we allow self to rule the relationship, and doing so will ultimately bring disappointment and pain. That is how I started at the airport. I wanted the crowd to serve my interests, never realizing that focus alone made them annoying instead of allowing me to see them the way Jesus did. For me to engage them in love, the focus had to shift from my wants, agenda, and needs to theirs. Perhaps the greatest freedom of one anothering is the freedom God gives us not to be focused on ourselves all the time. As I began to care about the people around me, I was set free from my own self-imposed deadline to enjoy the pageantry of human emotion going on around me.

Reality-based television shows are all the rage, because we find human drama engaging. But it is sad that we find more enjoyment in watching people in contrived circumstances than we do in engaging in the fascinating stories going on in our own neighborhoods, workplaces, and congregations, where amazing heroes are doing the right thing against incredible odds.

Jesus kept his focus on those around him, and it drove his disciples nuts. "Don't you want to go to Jerusalem and become famous?" they asked. They couldn't understand a Messiah who would spend the bulk of his time in Galilee, yet he wanted nothing more than to follow God's voice in loving people around him in the way they needed to be loved.

## Living Loved

Now we come to an important key for this and all the other one anothering Scriptures. We cannot do for others what hasn't already been done for us. Remember, Jesus' words to his disciples were to love one another *in the same way he had loved them.* His words hold true for you and me today. You cannot forgive others if you are not experiencing God's forgiveness for you. You cannot serve others unless you know that God is providing everything you need. You cannot live in kindness to others until you see God's kindness toward you. In that sense the one anothering Scriptures are less mandates to obey than they are descriptions of what love frees us to do. Such love does not begin in the human heart. It flows only from God himself, and he wants to fill you so that you are certain of his care for you in every detail of life. He will provide everything you need when you need it. That security in God's love is what will free you to live a one anothering life.

The more you experience the reality of God's love, the more you will find yourself sharing it with others. The last thing I want this book to do is to add to your list of ways a good Christian should act toward others. That misses the point. God doesn't want you to pretend to love others or to make you act like it. He wants to set you so free in his love that it spills out of you and touches others. It is an amazing process.

As you read through each aspect of one anothering, ask yourself how you see God exemplifying such treatment in your life. If you don't see it, ask him to show you. Believers quite naturally treat others the way they think God treats them, but often they don't clearly see what God is like. If you serve a God you think is judgmental with your sins, impatient with your weaknesses, and uninvolved in your pain, that is exactly how you will treat the people around you. My heart breaks for those who are caught in those traps. That's the God they live with every day.

Living in God's love is the first step to one anothering. If you don't discover that first, this process will wear you out with self-generated good works that will not bear the fruit of his kingdom. One anothering is not some onerous chore, but the joy of sharing God's life, not only with his people, but also with a world captive in darkness.

## The Fruits of One Anothering

Jesus said this simple command to love one another would bear fruit in two ways. First, it would demonstrate his reality to a world that cannot see him. "By this will all men know that you are my disciples, if you love one another" (John 13:35). There is no greater tool for touching the world than simple demonstrations of love. In fact, Jesus invited the world to judge the authenticity of the gospel we proclaim by the way we show love for others. That would be proof that we belong to him.

But that's not all. Jesus later added, "I have told you this so that my joy may be in you and that your joy may be complete" (John 15:11). Jesus' command for us to love one another was based in his desire for us to know his fullness. A self-centered life is its own punishment. When our relationships with others are filled with expectations and demands that they do what we want, the result is stress, disappointment, and despair. When God captures you with the reality of his love, you will be free to focus on others rather than on yourself. Here is where you will discover the joy of deep and abiding friendships. Jesus knew that. He knew that right relationships are the surest way to find fulfillment and freedom.

Throughout the chapters ahead I will show you how to build and develop friendships with other believers that will be transforming for you and for them. What may begin as a simple act of kindness can mature into a relationship in which you can share the highs and lows of your faith journey.

## The Greatest Is Love

"Love one another" is the ultimate one anothering Scripture. All the others are expressions of how we let God's love live out through us. They will show us how to express that love and expose to us the deepest treasures of what it means to be part of God's family. There are many "one another" and "each other" Scriptures I will not cover, but I have chosen these twenty-two verses as the ones most emphasized.

I have arranged them as they naturally flow through the early stages of a relationship to the deeper stages of friendship that body life can provide. However, please don't mistake this for a step-by-step program. Relationships are organic, and as such they develop best when an outside regimen is not imposed on them. Though deeper moments of honest confession often come only after people become comfortable in a relationship, I have had total strangers on a bus or in a store share with me some of their deepest struggles.

We will talk about ways you can be more intentional to build relationships, take them deeper, and then enjoy the depths of long-term friendships but be free to let them happen as God brings them about in your life. We will begin by looking on the inside where the foundation for Jesus-centered friendships is laid and see how, through forgiveness and preferring others, he frees us to engage people in a healthy way.

Next we'll look at the practical ways we open the door to new relationships: kindness, hospitality, and serving others. As we get to know one another better, we will find ourselves sharing our spiritual journeys through encouragement, counsel, and prayer. This involvement in one another's lives will put us in a place to help others through difficult and painful circumstances. We will learn how to stimulate people to see and choose God's best rather than fall to their own wisdom.

Finally, we will look at two wonderful possibilities that maturing relationships can add to our lives—the freedom to confess our faults and the safety of submitting to one another's wisdom and counsel.

At each stage of the process, keep an eye on how God demonstrates these actions toward you and the opportunities you have to love others in the same manner. This is the best of what the Christian life has to offer. Jump in and discover just how transforming a life lived in love can truly be.

## Discussion Questions

1. What are some of the things you learned in this chapter about Jesus' words "As I have loved you, so you must love one another"?
2. How would it change your day to look for individuals to love in the moment rather than to try to act like you love everybody?
3. In what ways have you treated others (or have had others treat you) that reflect how you (or they) thought about God?
4. Think through some of the encounters Jesus had with people when he walked this earth. Which one particularly stands out to you, and how did he demonstrate his Father's love to them?
5. In what ways would you like to see God's love demonstrated for you? Ask him to show you his love in that way.

# 3

# a soft place to fall

**. . . forgiving each other, just as in Christ God forgave you.**

*Ephesians 4:32*

**Accept one another, then, just as Christ accepted you.**

*Romans 15:7*

**. . . bearing with one another in love.**

*Ephesians 4:2*

Not forgiving is like swallowing rat poison and waiting for the rat to die.

Anne Lamott

If you were the woman in Scripture (John 8:1–11) who had been caught in the act of adultery, wouldn't you be grateful they dragged you to Jesus instead of to Caiaphas, the high priest, who had a dungeon in his basement?

Can you imagine what that woman must have been going through? Her life hung in the balance, and her accusers wanted her executed on the spot. But she was merely a pawn in the Pharisees' plan to force Jesus to abandon the grace and mercy he espoused or repudiate the law God had given. "In the Law Moses commanded us to stone such women. Now what do you say?" These Pharisees set their trap not suspecting that they had met their match. The man who had come showing God's amazing grace was the same God who had authored the law. There would be no contradiction here, only an opportunity for them to see clearly God's heart for people.

"If any one of you is without sin, let him be the first to throw a stone at her." How she must have tensed watching to see if any would pick up a stone. None did. Instead, they began to drift away. When none was left, Jesus turned again to her. "Woman, where are they? Has no one condemned you?"

"No one, sir," she said.

Little did she realize that the one remaining was without sin. By Jesus' own criterion he had the right to throw the first stone. But his words were as soft as they were loving: "Then neither do I condemn you. Go now and leave your life of sin" (v. 11).

At her worst moment this woman had fallen in the softest place. Others wanted to kill her, but the only one who had that right refused. In one incredible moment Jesus brought together all that God is in his holiness and all that we could be in his grace. When we experience that same mercy from him, we too will be as soft a place for people to fall as Jesus was.

## Unpacking Our Bags

Let's face it—relationships can be messy. When they're good, they're really good, but when relationships turn sour, nothing can be more painful. By first grade we learn how mean people can be and how they often will disappoint our greatest hopes. Being hurt by others can make us so judgmental and so protective of ourselves that it is difficult to invest in new relationships. Often the way someone looks or acts can trigger memories of an unpleasant person or experience, and if we haven't let go of the past, we will react by distancing ourselves from that person.

How are we ever going to connect at heart level when we are carrying that kind of baggage? Learning to deal with our past is critical to maintaining our friendships and opening up to new ones. Forgiveness and acceptance are the detergents of body life that allow us to live free of the past. Who doesn't need a fresh start now and then—the freedom to crawl out of old patterns and reputations to live in the newness of God's working? I remember leaving for college and starting out with an entirely new group of classmates. Nothing I had done in high school would matter. I relished that opportunity. Wouldn't it be great if life in the body of Christ could be that way every day?

Casual golfers often extend to one another what is called a "mulligan." After someone has hit a wayward shot deep into the woods or even out of bounds, his or her playing partners ignore the first shot so the player can hit another and play on without having to get out of trouble.

Jesus passed out a lot of mulligans. He constantly forgave people and encouraged them to do the same. He even linked God's forgiveness of us with ours for others. In one parable a man who had been forgiven a debt so huge he could never pay it turned around and demanded payment from a man who owed him a few pennies. Eventually this man ended up being thrown in prison himself. Jesus' parable points out how our ability to forgive others directly flows from the forgiveness we receive from God. When we see clearly the huge offenses he forgives in our lives, we surely will not want to hold others accountable to us for far less.

## Fellow Travelers

Competition subtly weaves its way into our friendships whenever we think we have to earn God's approval by our own will and effort. Since we all know in our most honest moments how far short we fall, we slip into the misguided hope that God might grade on the curve. I may not be perfect, but if I'm better than 90 percent of the Christians around me, then I'm sure I'll be safe.

That is not the way God thinks, but you can see how those who do think that way will regard other believers as competitors. Trying to be better than them, they will exaggerate the weaknesses of others while downplaying their own. True friendship cannot thrive in that environment. Jesus invited us not to live as competitors but as fellow travelers.

On the first day of their team-building retreat, coworkers were taken to the bottom of a mountain and divided into two teams. "The first one to get to the top of the hill wins," the instructor told them as he left to drive to the top of the mountain. The stronger soon left the weaker in their wake and after an hour or so began to arrive at the summit.

Each celebrated his or her success at getting to the top, not noticing that the instructor kept the stopwatch running. While they fought over who had won, the instructor kept looking down the rocky hillside. When the last member of the first team finally reached the top, he stopped his watch and announced the winning time at more than five hours.

"But I've been waiting up here for four hours," a member of the other team said. "I was the first one here."

"I wasn't referring to the first *person* to reach the summit, but the first *team*." As the instructor had planned, the participants felt cheated and wanted to restage the competition.

The next morning the coworkers went to the bottom of the mountain again. This time the teams were combined, and the only time that would matter is when the last person reached the summit. Now the stronger climbers did not rush ahead; instead, they stayed back to help those who were slow and uncertain climbing the rocks. In less than two hours, the entire group reached the summit together.

## A Truly Safe Place

Being a soft place to fall does not mean we become a doormat for everyone who wants to walk over us, nor that we ignore people's actions. Forgiving and accepting others simply means that we won't hold them accountable to us for their failures but will continue to respond to them with love and grace. Forgiveness frees us from the destruction others cause. It does not make us a further victim of it.

We can forgive someone who is abusive without continuing to subject ourselves to that abuse. And our forgiveness does not mean that we should keep silent if that person seeks to hurt others. Nor does our forgiveness absolve people of their responsibility, only of their accountability to us. If I forgive someone who commits a crime against me, that doesn't mean I will not seek justice to restrain that person from doing it to others. Forgiveness does not mean that we will forget what happened or pretend it didn't happen.

We are a soft place to fall when we love people through their failures and hurts as God draws them closer to himself and transforms them from within. We will still speak the truth firmly but will do so with gentleness and patience. One thing that has helped me with particularly difficult people is the realization that hurting people do stupid things. Usually the more stupidly they act, the deeper their pain. When someone lashes out at me or treats me with contempt, I am tempted to respond in kind. When I realize, however, that people who do such things are in incredible pain themselves, it helps me to be patient with them, hoping that my love and gentleness might open a door for their healing.

Learning to be quick to forgive, being ready to accept others where they are, and walking with them on their journey are three ways we begin the process of truly being a safe haven for others around us. That is why these one anothering Scriptures were key to life in the early church.

## "Forgiving One Another"

Forgiveness protects our relationships from the damage of the past. It frees others from the demand of perfection as it overlooks faults and offenses. When people learn to share the journey together, this process happens with hardly a thought. People who are constantly being forgiven by Jesus find it natural not to hold others to the standard they cannot meet themselves. By extending forgiveness to the adulteress, Jesus not only saved her from death but also gave her a chance to begin a new life.

Did she take it? We don't know. Many people confuse forgiveness and reconciliation, which are two entirely different processes. Forgiveness is a unilateral act. It does not absolve someone from sin, but it does free that person from my judgment and vengeance. Forgiving the hurts of others is essential to my own personal health. By releasing others from my desire for retribution, I can live free of bitterness and overcome hurts others have caused.

Reconciliation, however, is a process of healing between the offender and the offended. Reconciliation demands that the offender recognize his or her offense, understand the pain it caused, offer restitution to whatever degree possible, and offer some assurance that the offending pattern will change. Often the offense is not one-sided; both parties contribute to each other's offense.

Though reconciliation is always preferable, it is not always possible, because the person who offended you may not see his or her actions in the same light as you do. While it is always worth the effort to see if reconciliation is possible, we are still free to forgive whether or not the offender ever acknowledges his failure. When Jesus forgave his executioners and the mockers who surrounded him on the cross, he refused to allow their selfishness to incite him to respond similarly. Rather than react to their abusiveness, he found his way into the freedom of forgiveness.

For the body of Christ to stay relationally healthy, we will need to jump freely and often into the waters of forgiveness. We all are works in progress overcoming different weaknesses. The better we know one another the more we will need to overlook, but the rewards of doing so are great. Don't be discouraged when forgiveness doesn't come easily. Forgiveness itself is less a choice than it is a process. Yes, we do choose to forgive, but often it takes a work of God in our heart to lead us into the full depth and freedom of no longer holding something against someone else.

## "Accepting One Another"

A few years ago I sat in a roomful of believers and was struck by the desperate circumstances that plagued so many of us—a wife whose husband had committed suicide, a set of parents at the end of their rope with their children, two people experiencing great difficulties with their jobs, and one man falsely accused of using his work computer to download pornography. A couple of years earlier, I had been forced out of a church staff position by my then best friend, and now I was helping my wife care for her two terminally ill parents at home.

As I made note of the great needs in that room, I remarked that this seemed so different from a few years before when my wife and I hardly knew anyone going through such struggles. "What's going on?" I asked, wondering if we were involved in some conspiracy of evil to torment the body of Christ.

Knowing looks flashed about the room. "Should we tell him?" one of them asked.

"It's not we who've changed," he continued. "A few years ago you weren't safe for hurting people to be around. You had all the answers and would try to help people by giving them advice to fix it, never realizing that what you said wasn't helpful. Now that you've been through some difficult times yourself, you are a much safer person for people to stay near."

I felt embarrassed that my weaknesses were so obvious to others, but that explained something that had always bothered me as a pastor. Whenever we held workshops to help strengthen marriages, the wrong people would always show up. Those with good marriages would come to make them better. Those who were struggling, the very people for whom we had planned these events, always had good excuses to stay away. I thought it was because they weren't serious about God's work in them. I didn't know I wasn't a safe place to fall. They wanted help, but what I was doing to prod them forward wasn't helpful.

Accept people just as they are, trusting that God will change them in time. Accepting them as people does not mean you condone their behavior or beliefs. It simply means you respect their humanity enough to let them work through the process. People open their lives to those who accept them the way they are and run from those who are always trying to change them into what they think they should be.

## "Bearing with One Another"

How many times I've sat across the room from someone going through extremely painful circumstances and been at a complete loss as to how to help them! I used to feel worthless if I couldn't fix the problem. Now I know that fixing the problem isn't what people need most. Over the years the most helpful thing I've said to people in pain is simply this: "I want you to know, no matter how bad this gets, I will be here for you."

Sometimes that isn't easy. When my brother was dying of multiple sclerosis, even some of his closest friends stopped coming to visit. "I just can't stand to see him that way," they would say. Ninety percent of love is being there—being a comforting presence even when it isn't easy. That presence more than anything defines how God treats us. We can offer it to others as well.

I remember at one point being involved in a venture for which my paycheck was never certain. Though I sensed it was the right thing to do, I often wondered what I'd do if it failed. One day a dear friend who had a successful career pulled me aside and said, "As long as my family has a place to sleep and food to eat, so will yours." I can't tell you how much that set me at ease. Though I never needed to take him up on his offer, just knowing that he would be there gave me the courage to press on.

Isn't that true of God's presence in our own lives? To know that I cannot earn his love and that he will endure with me even through my most difficult days gives me all the grace I need to hang in there and let him sort things out. Imagine how powerful it is when we model that for others.

## Discussion Questions

1. If you hadn't known how Jesus handled the situation, how would you have treated the woman caught in adultery?
2. How could your group be a softer place for people to fall?
3. Where do you find yourself competing with other believers, and what will help put an end to that?
4. Think of a time when someone forgave you for a specific offense or loved you through some broken moment in your life. How did that make you feel?
5. Tell about a time when someone stood by you through a difficult season in your life. How are you doing that now for someone, or how do you need it?

# 4

# it's not all about you

**Be devoted to one another.**

*Romans 12:10*

**Honor one another above yourselves.**

*Romans 12:10*

Selfishness is not living as one wishes to live, it is asking others to live as one wishes to live.

Oscar Wilde

I don't know how you do it," I said shaking my head. "I think I would be bored out of my mind teaching the same material every week."

On the other side of the table was Gayle Erwin, author of *The Jesus Style,* who for the past twenty-five years has taught almost the same seminar every weekend on the nature of Jesus. He even jokes about traveling the world playing his one-string guitar. As one who relished the challenge of finding fresh material every week for the same crowd, I couldn't imagine teaching similar material to different crowds every week.

His reply was far gentler than his words appear in print. With a twinkle in his eye and a smile forming on his lips, he responded, "Oh, so ministry is still about you!"

His simple statement has challenged and blessed me ever since. I had been schooled in environments where ministry was about my gifts, my abilities, my passions, and my vision. It is amazing how blind we can be when our lives orbit around our needs and desires. As long as friendship and ministry are all about you and what you want or need, you will find yourself getting further away from them even as you try harder to cultivate them.

We were in the middle of an eye-opening discussion on Matthew 5 when Jill interrupted with a question: "Can we talk about me now?" She is a single mom in a dead-end job with a desperate desire for friendship and few friends to show for it. She is so focused on herself that even those who want to know her quickly grow weary.

Most of us are usually subtler, but the result is the same. Like a spinning merry-go-round on the playground, a self-focused life will unwittingly push others away. If we are going to participate in the joy of one anothering, we need to let Jesus rewire our thinking so that we are even more aware of others than we are of ourselves.

## Not Here for Me

If anyone deserved to be the center of attention and to demand that others serve his needs, it was Jesus. He was God after all. He had created the world, given life and breath to his disciples, chosen them out of the world, and would soon be executed for their redemption. If he had demanded they serve his every whim, no one would have deserved it more.

But he didn't.

"For even the Son of Man did not come to be served, but to serve, and to give his life as a ransom for many" (Mark 10:45). Do you remember the context of those words? Jesus had just told his disciples that he was going to Jerusalem to be beaten and crucified (vv. 33–34). You would think the disciples would have expressed their concern for him in the face of the horrible events ahead. They didn't; they were too busy thinking about themselves. James and John saw time running out in their quest to be at the top. Instead of responding to Jesus' need, they asked him for the best seats in his kingdom. The rest weren't any better, for they grew indignant with James and John because they had asked first.

What a superb time for a lesson on ministry! Most people treat others as their servants, trying to get out of them whatever they need to be happy. Jesus wanted his followers to understand that just the opposite was true in his kingdom. Even he had not come to make people meet his needs but to be available to touch theirs. If there is a secret to the fulfilled and fruitful life in Christ, this is it. But this reverses every one of our natural inclinations. No matter what circumstance we encounter, we are naturally focused on our own needs and desires, trying to maximize any gain or minimize any pain. That is why selfish actions and defense mechanisms kick in with hardly any forethought.

This struggle to satisfy self, however, is our greatest tyranny. Instead of relaxing in the moment, we constantly have to manipulate it. We find ourselves using people instead of loving them. If the one who had the right to demand that kind of attention refused it to give his life away to others, what more do we need to know?

Changing the focus from us to others, however, doesn't happen by mere choice. Trying to put everyone else's needs above our own will wear us out. Those who try it eventually revert to looking out for themselves because, as we all know, if we don't take care of ourselves, no one else will. Or do we?

A life lived in love will only work out of a growing trust in God to provide for us and show us how to love people he has put near us.

## Who's Got My Back?

The best moments in marriage don't come when each partner is looking out for his or her own rights, but when each partner looks after the interests of the other. Instead of each having to manipulate the other to be fulfilled, each looks out for the other's needs and desires.

We will never spin free of orbiting around our own self-interest by ignoring our concerns; we must allow God to take care of them. Jesus could go through life responding to others around him because he trusted that God would look after him. He didn't have to walk into circumstances protecting himself or trying to get his way. He knew his Father would provide everything he needed.

What an incredible freedom! Many people live their whole lives never discovering the joy of trusting God to take care of them. When you know that your whole life is in God's hands and that he can provide everything you need, you no longer have to fight for things at someone else's expense. You will find yourself relaxed enough to actually do the things that can bless someone else.

I used to be a task-oriented person, always with something to do and an agenda in every circumstance. Looking back, I think my whole countenance screamed, "Leave me alone; I'm busy!" because that is exactly what people did. Social scientists tell us that 93 percent of communication is nonverbal. No matter how much we may tell people we want to help, our demeanor may be screaming that we don't.

In recent years, however, I have been finding just the opposite happening. As I am learning to trust Jesus to take care of me, I am less stressed about what I have to do, and people seem to pick up that I am more available. While on jury duty last summer, I was waiting with three hundred other people to be called to a courtroom. As people scattered throughout the courthouse, I sat alone in a row of chairs reading a book. A few moments later I noticed a young woman in a short, tight skirt turn into my row and walk past twenty vacant chairs to sit in the one right next to mine.

Since I am nearly fifty, I thought it a bit strange. I turned to her, and we chatted briefly. When the conversation lulled I turned back to my book. "Can I ask you something?" Her voice had turned serious. She told me about a horrible fight she had had with her father the night before and how angry it had made her.

Being a father of a young woman her age, I was able to walk through the conversation with her and point out what I would have meant if I'd said similar things to my daughter. I explained to her how fathers think and told her that what she saw as an unwelcome intrusion may have been her father's attempt at expressing his love for her. Since I didn't know her father, I told her I could be wrong, but it was clear she didn't think so. She thanked me and told me she would go by and visit her dad that night to clear things up.

At the end of the conversation, I even asked about her relationship with her heavenly Dad. Before she got called out to a courtroom, I told her that as much as her dad loved her, God loved her even more. She had no idea what I was saying, but I planted a seed in her that might blossom someday.

## The Ruse of Expectations

Jesus could have been devastated by the fact that in the face of his death the disciples cared only about their positions in his future kingdom. But he wasn't. He knew the selfishness that dominates most human relationships and was already past their failure before they were. In fact, nothing seemed to bother him about his friends—not when Martha thought kitchen chores were more important than conversing with him, not when Peter denied him at trial, and not when Thomas doubted his resurrection.

Jesus didn't lace his relationships with expectations, and he refused to be trapped when others sought to put their expectations on him. He disappointed Mary and Martha by delaying his trip to Bethany when they begged him to come and heal their brother, Lazarus. He didn't tell people all they wanted to know, nor did he heal people just to prove his power. Many misunderstood him, and others got angry with him, yet he just kept loving them as they were, gently pointing them to the truth and letting them decide whether to come or not. He refused to manipulate people even for their own good, and he was not crushed when they turned on him.

The popular saying is true: "Expectations are resentments waiting to happen." We sabotage many of our relationships by imposing expectations on others or trying to meet theirs. It cannot be done. People who live with expectations will never be satisfied. Of course we can still love those who impose their expectations on us, but we will also have to find peace in knowing that we may never be able to love them in the way they demand it.

Gilbert had been in the hospital for a few days, and since I had been out of town, I had not gotten by to see him sooner. When I did, all he could do was complain about how lonely he had been. No one had come by to see him. No one cared about him. As I heard him talk, I knew better. I knew at least half a dozen people who had told me they had come by to see him.

"Gilbert, are you sure?" I finally asked him. "Didn't Marty come by a few days ago, and Mark, Jim, and Paul too?"

He cocked his head remembering. I honestly didn't think he was lying to me. He had been so wrapped up in his disappointment that I hadn't come, he couldn't appreciate the others who had. That is what expectations do. They make us look for the person we want to help us instead of letting God send whomever he desires.

Disappointments are the surest test that you are a captive to expectations. When you hear yourself saying, "If they loved me, they wouldn't (or would) have . . ." or "After all I've done for them, you'd think. . . ," know that you've fallen into a trap from which there is only one escape. Instead of letting your disappointment rage at whoever has not done what you thought he or she should, ask Jesus to help you trust him to bring whoever you need into your life without demanding that it come your way.

## "Be Devoted to One Another"

The first of our two one anothering Scriptures that will help us get our eyes off ourselves is the call to be "devoted to one another." I've often heard this phrase used to encourage believers to be committed to one another. For the last two thousand years, the church has been passionate about commitment. Church membership, home group participation, and even covenant relationships have been used to attempt to promote healthy relationships between believers.

Certainly Paul knew that relationships of convenience would never mean much, but he didn't see commitment as the answer. In fact, you will not find the word *commitment* anywhere in the New Testament; and you will only find the word *commit* when it encourages us *not* to commit adultery or acts of wickedness. The word translated "devoted" in this passage is a relational word that speaks of having kindly affection for others. When we substitute something like commitment for affection, we mistake the shadow for the reality. As we experience God's affection for us, we will find ourselves having affection in our hearts for others.

That doesn't mean we will have this affection for everyone we meet. We would be exhausted with busyness if we did. But in the course of your journey, you will find those with whom God makes a connection. You will find affection in your heart for them. This won't include only people who are easy to love; God will also give you affection for those trapped in deep bondage or need. Out of those relationships we may find ourselves walking more intentionally with a group of brothers and sisters, either as part of a congregation, mission team, or fellowship group. Most enduring friendships are formed in small-group environments where people share the Christian life for a season. I have always tried to have a small group of ten to twelve with whom I regularly walk in openness and honesty, and that has yielded some extraordinary fruit in my life.

Once I was complaining to one of those groups that I had to be out of town on Saturday morning the first time my son would get to start at quarterback for his fifth-grade flag football team. He had been second-string but was moved up that day because the regular quarterback was out of town. I had visions of my son in therapy for years because his dad missed his first start in a football game.

When I called my son that Saturday afternoon to find out how the game had gone, he told me that the game had been stopped in the third quarter because his team was ahead 38 to 0. "You know what else, Dad?" he added. "A whole bunch of people showed up to watch me." At 7:30 on a Saturday morning, half of that home group had showed up to take my place along the sidelines. You can't get "committed" people to do that. They were there because they cared about Andy and me, and neither one of us has ever forgotten it.

"Let no debt remain outstanding, except the continuing debt to love one another" (Rom. 13:8). If we learn to love one another, we will need nothing more. We won't need commitment, we won't fall victim to expectations, and we won't be disappointed when others don't do for us what we have done for them. God's love demands nothing in return. What you will find is that for every thirty or forty people you love like that, one or two just might respond with similar concern for you. These are the ones with whom you will get to experience a depth of spiritual community that is unrivaled by anything else in this world.

## "Honor One Another above Yourselves"

Honoring others above ourselves simply means to put their needs above our own and watch out for their well-being. Paul tells us that the stronger we are in faith, the freer we will be to defer to the needs of the weaker. How would that ever work in an institutional setting? All of our procedures are set up to make sure that the stronger lead us in the right way so that those who are weaker can't ruin it. Any other way would result in chaos, many argue.

That would appear to be true, but this is Christ's body, after all, and he has ways of using even the struggles of the weak to lead the body into greater depths of transformation. Jesus was more concerned with building healthy relationships than stable institutions. Entering a room and not demanding what we want but being ready to help others get what they need is the essence of genuine church life.

Can you imagine what body life would look like if everyone came to be a blessing to others? It would revolutionize church life. In the average congregation today, 10 percent of the people fulfill 90 percent of the responsibility. That is because we have been schooled as consumers, finding fellowship where we get our needs met—where we get fed, have the worship experience we prefer, unload our guilt, have our children discipled, and maybe even gather business contacts.

Consumers will never discover the joy of Christian community. As long as we orbit around our own needs, we will miss the freedom of preferring others. Consumers will never know the joy of taking the last place in line at a potluck, helping make sure every mess is cleaned up before they leave, caring more about how someone heard it than how they said it, nor giving up a personal want for someone else's need.

Can you imagine how a group of people who honor others above themselves would make God's love known in a self-preferring world? It can happen so simply. When God has so satisfied you that you can trust him to fulfill every hunger in your life, you are ready to experience the depths of one anothering. These first few chapters have set the foundation by which we can open our lives to people God brings near us. Now we will look at how these relationships get started and grow over time and then at how maturing relationships open the greatest treasures of friendship.

## Discussion Questions

1. Have you ever destroyed a good relationship by trying to force your own way?

2. Think of two people in your life who loved you with no expectations in return. How did that make you feel? What kind of relationship did you have with them?
3. Suggest some ways your group could grow in being devoted to one another through affection, not commitment.
4. What are some practical ways you can honor others above yourselves in this group on a regular basis?

# Part 2

## opening the door

Every friend you have today was once a stranger who crossed your path. Friendships begin in simple moments offered by a warm smile, a gentle word, or a kind act. They open the way for us to discover the treasures God has placed around us.

# 5

# initial contact

**Greet one another.**

*2 Corinthians 13:12*

**Offer hospitality to one another.**

*1 Peter 4:9*

You can make more friends in two months by becoming interested in other people than you can in two years by trying to get other people interested in you.

Dale Carnegie

Hello.
How are you?
G'day.
Hey!
Howdy!
Good to see you!
Aloha!
Whazzup?

We have many colorful ways to great one another, often depending on where we live, but how sincere are they?

A popular commercial illustrates this perfectly. A Texan, donned in a cowboy hat, enters a bar in New York where he is greeted by a man with a nod and "How ya doin'?" in his definitive Brooklyn accent.

The Texan smiles and responds with a rich southern drawl: "Well, I'm doin' just fine. Thank ya for askin'. I just got into town. . . ." Then he launches into a detailed description about his day.

The New Yorkers roll their eyes. A couple of men shooting pool pause, eyebrows raised and heads shaking, as if to say, "What a moron!" Then the door opens and a local patron walks into the establishment. He walks up to the bar, plants himself on an empty stool next to the Texan, and mutters, "How ya doin'?"

The room groans as the Texan swivels his stool toward the man and starts again, "Well, I'm doin' just fine. Thank ya for askin'. . . ."

Who of us in the midst of a hectic day hasn't offered a polite, "How are you?" only to cringe as the person begins to lay out the status of his life and of everyone in his family? That is what makes this commercial amusing—it strikes a familiar chord.

Greetings are often only a social courtesy. We do not expect someone to take us seriously and launch into a detailed conversation, especially with a stranger. But greetings are actually more important than we realize. Congregations look for their friendliest members to place at the entrance so that visitors feel welcome. I have a good friend who had a passion for being the best greeter at the congregation we attended years ago. He took this very seriously, even spending a year being mentored by an older gentleman who had the process down pat. He learned to smile warmly, to shake hands with just the right firmness, and to know where everything was in the facility so that he could give the right directions to young families looking for Sunday school rooms for their children. He has a wonderful heart to greet people, but Scripture's encouragement to greet one another is not a ministry for a few—it is a way of life for us all.

## Where Relationships Begin

Most relationships begin with a simple greeting offered sincerely. It can begin a conversation, which in turn can start a friendship that can powerfully affect both lives.

We generally don't take our greetings that seriously, do we? The New Testament letters are filled with references to greeting, and five of them even mention doing it with a kiss. How would that go over next time you ran into someone at your fellowship?

Yes, I know there is a cultural difference between first-century Israel and the Western civilization many of us live in today. But even today in the Middle East the customary greeting for men involves grasping each other's right hand while placing the left hand on the other man's right shoulder and exchanging kisses on each cheek. Women often greet each other in a similar way, but men and women do not kiss as a casual greeting. Nor do strangers practice this type of greeting. Thus, Scripture indicates that early believers were deeply involved in one another's lives. It was a natural thing for Paul and Peter to encourage them to greet one another warmly, as they would if they were close friends or family—for they were.

With today's busy lives and overbooked schedules, we feel taxed just to give a polite "Hello" or a quick "Good to see you" as we rush through our day. How often do we stop to think of the rare treasure we might miss in passing?

In chapter 2 we talked about living a life focused on others. The most powerful way that begins is by simply showing an interest in somebody else's life with a sincere greeting and then taking the time to listen to the response. You'll be amazed at some of the reactions you'll get and how quickly the door can open to a new friendship.

## A Greeting That Changed a Life

"Will you give me a drink?" Jesus asked a woman as she approached Jacob's well near Sychar in Samaria (John 4:7). It was an unusual greeting that defied cultural norms, but Jesus was interested in engaging her in a conversation that might open the window of her soul to his indescribable gift.

The woman was taken aback. "You are a Jew and I am a Samaritan woman. How can you ask me for a drink?" (John 4:9).

If Jesus had followed the dictates of society, he never would have reached this woman. Instead, he engaged her on a level she had never experienced before even with a fellow Samaritan, much less a Jew. That greeting not only surprised her but also opened the door to a conversation that allowed Jesus to reveal his Father's heart for her in the midst of her brokenness. When they finished, she gathered her relatives so they could hear him, and many Samaritans in that town believed simply because Jesus took an interest in one woman.

Having a freelance career in television production gives me an opportunity to see colleagues I may not have seen in some time. A number of them, Christian and non-Christian alike, respond to my greeting, "How are things?" by seeking out time during the day to delve into a discussion about the stresses and strains of their lives. Often these moments lead to my sharing about Jesus and even praying with them. During these impromptu encounters, their openness with their personal struggles often surprises me. I think they are open because over the years I have shown genuine interest in them.

## Imparting a Blessing

Beyond inquiring about someone's life, greetings can also impart God's blessings. In the book of Ruth, Boaz returned home from a trip and went to a field where his crew was harvesting. He greeted them with, "The LORD be with you!" To which they replied, "The LORD bless you" (2:4).

Paul, in the opening of nearly every one of his epistles, proclaimed, "Grace and peace to you from God our Father and from the Lord Jesus Christ" or some close variation (see, e.g., Rom. 1:7; 1 Cor. 1:3; 2 Cor. 1:2). Peter wrote, "Grace and peace be yours in abundance," in his letters (1 Peter 1:2; 2 Peter 1:2). John used language like "Grace, mercy and peace from God the Father and from Jesus Christ" (2 John 3) and "I pray that you may enjoy good health and that all may go well with you" (3 John 2).

I can picture the disciples using similar words as they greeted one another in person. Perhaps the early church used words of greeting like these even as they embraced and kissed. What a wonderful way to encourage one another and affirm God's blessing together! It sure makes "Whazzup?" or "How ya doin'?" seem flippant by comparison.

Of course, using such over-the-top language may seem a bit pretentious in our day, but there are simpler ways we can express joy and blessing to others, even as a heartfelt prayer for them.

## Guess Who's Coming to Dinner?

When my family moved to Tennessee several years ago, I was told that I wouldn't be able to step into a congregation without being invited over to somebody's house for lunch. It's great that southern hospitality has such a wonderful reputation, and my family did find the people friendly as we grew to love Nashville, but we were not invited into anyone's home for a meal for more than a year after we started attending a local fellowship.

And these were friendly people! We felt welcomed in the fellowship and got to know different families as time went on, but we were never approached to join someone at their home for a meal. Dinner fellowship is becoming much too rare in the body of Christ these days, and that is tragic, since hospitality is one of the ways we turn a greeting into a relationship. Inviting people for a meal and an evening in our home creates an opportunity to get to know them better. The first Christians did it quite often. As a matter of fact, the early church flourished in the homes of believers. Acts 2:46 says, "They broke bread in their homes and ate together with glad and sincere hearts."

The home provides the perfect setting for relationships to get beyond the superficial and head into deeper waters. Friendships begin and take hold in such environments where we have the time to explore one another's lives. If you lack the kind of relationships you desire, look at how often you invite people into extended opportunities for relationship.

My brother-in-law lives in a small desert community in Nevada. We joke that Joe doesn't know a stranger. Whenever we visit him and his wife, we never know how many people will be at their house for dinner. Guests may include any of a number of their friends who happen to drop by or even someone they just met. Joe's place is always open, and they have a wonderful attitude about hospitality—it doesn't have to be perfect. What you see is what you get.

I know too many people who shy away from hospitality because they think their home has to be spotless and the meal scrumptious. The whole point of opening the door to new friendships is not to impress people but to be real. If we don't break away from the need to put on our best face, we will never develop genuine relationships. Everything doesn't have to be perfect. We can order pizza, throw hot dogs on the grill, or make sandwiches. What's important is unhurried time together to let people see into our lives.

## Deeper Still

My oldest daughter is thirteen years old, and she has been asking to have her friends spend the night at our house since she was five. Now our youngest is beginning to do the same thing. I ask them why they need to have a sleepover when they see their friends at school every day. Their reply: "We get to know them so much better than we can at school."

I can't argue with that. There is something about spending significant time together that opens the door to deeper relationships. In my work with small groups, I have noticed that one weekend retreat with a few people can advance relationships four to six months. People get beyond the easy conversations about family, jobs, and congregational activities and begin to let people see who they really are.

My wife and I returned to Nashville recently for a couple of days. We spent each night at the home of a different couple—friends who were already dear to us. Yet that simple act made the relationships that much sweeter. Think of what we would have missed if we had spent those nights in a hotel.

Finding the time to develop relationships isn't easy in our busy culture, but if we don't, we will continue to feel isolated. What good would it do for us to greet friends, sincerely asking how they are doing, only to cut off their reply because we are late for an appointment? Friendships only grow as we make time available to them. Sociologists tell us that it takes three interpersonal contacts a week for a relationship to grow. If we want to live a life of one anothering, we will have to tackle our struggles with time.

## Leaving Room in the Margins

Richard A. Swenson, in his book *Margin: How to Create the Emotional, Physical, Financial, and Time Reserves You Need,* shows us that stress and burnout result when people don't leave any margin in their lives. They fill up every available space with job, family responsibilities, and recreational pursuits and have nothing left in reserve for unexpected crisis or opportunity.

Our lives need margins, just like the space at the edge of these pages. Living marginless is getting to work thirty minutes late because you left the house fifteen minutes after you had planned to because your daughter didn't get her math homework completed. Then you discovered that your gas tank was empty, so you stopped and put in only five dollars' worth of gas so you wouldn't arrive even later.

Opportunity for deepening friendships often comes in unanticipated moments. We may be missing a lot of one anothering moments simply because we are too busy to engage others meaningfully. How do we overcome that?

Prayerfully take a look at how busy you are, and remember that you don't have to fill the needs of everybody around you. As we learned earlier, God wants us to love "one at a time." If at this point you are stressing over a simple greeting or an invitation to dinner, it might be time to reconsider how you spend your time. Simple adjustments in your schedule and attitude can allow you the freedom to capitalize on one anothering opportunities.

Don't think of one anothering as one more onerous chore to add to all your other obligations. Look for ways to add people to the things you already do—hobbies, errand running, household projects, and other activities—and experience the joy of fellowship.

## You Never Know . . .

"Keep on loving each other as brothers. Do not forget to entertain strangers, for by so doing some people have entertained angels without knowing it" (Heb. 13:1–2). When I'm traveling, I often stay in the homes of the people that invited me to come and share with them. I often leave a note that says something like, "I wish I could tell you that you've entertained an angel unaware, but, alas, it was just me. . . ."

The next person you have over for dinner probably won't be an angel either, but be careful; you never know whom God will send your way to bless your life or for you to bless.

Take a look around you and see where you can be hospitable. Then clear your schedule and invite a friend or somebody you may not know well over for lunch or dinner. It sounds easy—because it is! It's often the first step to a priceless friendship.

## Discussion Questions

1. How do you normally greet people? Do you expect a real answer?
2. What can you do to make your greetings more sincere?

3. Read the example of Jesus with the Samaritan woman in John 4. How can we step out of the normal pattern of greeting and open a door into people's lives?
4. What practical ways can you suggest to practice hospitality?
5. How are the margins of your life? Share some ideas that would open up more space in your weekly schedule.

# 6

# sharing god's kindness

**Be kind and compassionate to one another.**

*Ephesians 4:32*

**Share with others.**

*Hebrews 13:16*

Kind words can be short and easy to speak, but their echoes are truly endless.

Mother Teresa

The first time Jason and Eileen knocked on their new neighbors' door across the street, they were dismissed with a wave and a shout. When they explained who they were, the older couple apologized and let them in. "We thought you were more Jehovah's Witnesses," they explained.

In the next few moments, Jason and Eileen learned how angry these neighbors were after having lived next to a growing fellowship in Southern California. Their yard had been trampled and their driveway blocked by people attending services. For years they had refused offers from the fellowship to buy their home. One night, they said, the people had even marched around their home singing and praying, claiming their property for God. The marchers terrified them, because the couple had no idea what the marchers were doing, and the next day they found their yard completely trampled. They eventually moved out of the city to a spot on this country road.

It wasn't long before the couple found out Jason was a pastor, and they told him in no uncertain terms that they never wanted him to speak to them about his faith. "I promise you," Jason responded, "I'll never talk with you about my faith until you ask me."

Over the next few years, the two couples periodically exchanged greetings across the street and sometimes exchanged mail that had been delivered to the wrong house. Though the relationship was cordial, Jason and Eileen prayed for an opportunity to help their neighbors see beyond the abuse they had suffered. Five years later an opening came. While picking up the mail one day, Jason discovered a bill intended for his neighbors. He walked over, and noticing their paper still on the driveway, picked it up too and took it to their door.

"You haven't gotten out to get the paper yet today?" Jason asked the wife when she answered the door.

"We just can't get it ourselves anymore." Their deteriorating medical conditions prevented them from walking to the end of their hundred-foot driveway. "My son brings it to us when he comes by after work."

Jason's response was immediate. "What if I bring your paper over every morning when I get mine?" The woman told him not to bother, but he could tell it would be a blessing to them. For the next seven years, Jason or Eileen picked up their neighbors' paper in the morning, walked it up their driveway, and set it on their back porch.

That simple act opened a huge door. The conversations that ensued during that time through casual chatter, medical emergencies, and neighborhood issues allowed a friendship to blossom, and finally the neighbors asked Jason and Eileen to share what they knew about Jesus. Eventually they came to believe as well, and when the husband passed away, Jason was asked to officiate at his funeral. A simple act of kindness repeated over the years had washed away the anger and softened their hearts to the gospel.

## Kindness in a Selfish Age

In a culture where most people are looking out for number one, random acts of kindness stand out as brightly as a lighthouse on a moonless night. You can see mistrust in people's eyes when you offer to help them for no reason.

"What's in it for you?" they ask. The answer is nothing from their perspective but everything from God's perspective. For Jason and Eileen to take the newspaper each morning was not a cumbersome task. However, it was enough to turn what could have been a sour relationship and a source of stress in the neighborhood into a friendship. Kindness does that; it is a powerful reality.

Earlier chapters have given us the groundwork for living a life focused on others. Now it's time to experience the joy in doing so. The quote above from Mother Teresa is profound: "Kind words can be short and easy to speak, but their echoes are truly endless." And it's not just kind words, either. Kind actions, though often quick and easy to accomplish, can echo eternally as well.

When you walk through your day focused on others, you will be amazed at the opportunities you might otherwise miss. Give directions to somebody who looks lost, help a neighbor working in the yard, offer to watch a friend's child while your friend is in the hospital, stay and help clean up after a home group meeting, let somebody step in front of you in line at the grocery store, or deliver a cold drink to a carpenter working in your attic. I could spend the rest of this chapter offering suggestions of how we can be kind to one another, but you will see them yourself when you have an eye focused on others.

While greeting and hospitality can open the door to relationships, acts of kindness and sharing can take them much further.

## Breaking the Cycle

The Scriptures that tell us to be kind to one another don't stand alone. They are tied to situations where people have been hurt or wonged. In Ephesians 4:31, Paul admonishes, "Get rid of all bitterness, rage and anger, brawling and slander, along with every form of malice." He adds in 1 Thessalonians 5:15, "Make sure that nobody pays back wrong for wrong, but always try to be kind to each other and to everyone else." That is not how we normally act when wronged. Paul, however, encourages us not to do to others as they have done unto us—not to pay back wrong for wrong. We aren't to allow anger or bitterness to find a place in our hearts.

But Paul doesn't stop there; he gives us something positive to do—be kind. Showing kindness breaks the cycle. It is our nature to hold a grudge. If somebody does something to us, we keep an account and look for a way to get even someday. Payback is sweet. Or we may think we are doing well just to ignore and stay away from the person who has offended us. At least we haven't tried to get even. But as God's children we live under a different priority. When you have been wronged, instead of reciprocating and feuding like the Hatfields and McCoys, look for ways to be kind and see the miracle of one anothering unfold.

When I was in college, I had the opportunity to play in a Christian band. We traveled on weekends doing concerts and spent our summers on the road ministering in congregations throughout the United States. It was a wonderful experience that proved to be life changing for all of us. Jim, the lead guitar player, was a character—a hockey player with fingers as big as tree stumps. To this day I don't see how he played the way he did.

Jim and I came from different backgrounds, and we didn't see eye to eye on many things—especially music. On a natural level, we never would have been friends. That first summer I was struggling with our relationship. Spending three months together wore me down—and I'm sure him as well. Our conflicts were nothing major, but we did irritate each other. With some wise advice from another member of our band, I started practicing being kind whenever I felt offended by or angry with him. I coupled that with focusing on Jim's good qualities, of which there were many. It didn't happen overnight, but things did begin to change. What had begun as a strained relationship blossomed into a full-fledged friendship—one that continues to this day.

I have in-laws in the same city where Jim now lives. We are able to get together about once a year and have lunch or play golf. I cherish our relationship, which is the fruit of Paul's admonition not to pay back wrong for wrong but instead to discover the power of kindness.

## Living in Generosity

Brenda was going through a rough time in her life. She was in the midst of a painful divorce, raising two children alone, and she was strapped with a large financial burden from her soon-to-be former husband.

Norma, who worked with Brenda in the office of their fellowship in Oklahoma, took notice of Brenda's situation. She would often take Brenda to lunch, and their relationship grew as they spent time together. Often when Brenda would put her coat on at the end of the day, she would find a twenty-dollar bill stuffed into her pocket. She never asked where it came from, but in her own words: "I always suspected Norma. The wisdom she gently and lovingly shared still remains with me today, though our conversations and her ministry to me occurred almost twenty years ago. God used Norma to show me love and real friendship when I was so love-starved and lonely. She truly 'held up my arms' during that time, and I will never forget it."

We will only be free to share the way Norma did when we view our possessions in a new light. Nothing we own is really ours. Everything belongs to God. If we are trusting God to supply our needs, then it makes sense that we should readily share what God has given us with others we encounter along the way. And sharing doesn't stop with money. It includes our time, our home, and our possessions.

Institutional ways of helping those in need always break down. Personally helping those God has placed in our path doesn't. Don't be concerned with the tax repercussions. God will more than make up for your generosity. You can't outgive him. The early church in Acts regularly shared what they had so that no one would be in need. Look at your assets as gifts from God, and be free to pass them on when he asks. As you discover how generous he is with you, you will find the joy of being generous with others.

I have a friend who puts a set amount of cash in his pocket each month with the specific intent of looking for people he can bless with it. He has learned to freely share what he has with others, and it has opened unbelievable doors for him to share Jesus. People who would have rejected the four spiritual laws or an invitation to a church service have opened up to him because of his generosity.

A good friend of mine in Tennessee had a rough start with the new pastor that had been brought on board in his fellowship. Through some difficult meetings and confrontations over church government issues, their relationship was strained. Philip wasn't a rich man, but one day he felt like God laid it on his heart to buy his pastor a new suit. Being a sensible man, this seemed rather odd, but Philip followed through.

He called up the pastor and asked him to meet him during his lunch hour. The pastor did and was surprised when Philip took him to a men's clothing store. In a few minutes, the pastor had been fitted with a new suit. The pastor didn't want to accept the gift—especially coming from someone he viewed as his enemy. But Philip persisted.

The two never came to agreement on church government, but I believe Philip's obedience to God allowed the pastor to see that their disagreement was not personal. He was still loved by his brother in Christ. An act of kindness like that in the midst of conflict is a powerful way to follow the first one anothering Scripture—*love one another.*

## You Did It for Me

More than anything else, Jesus said our acts of kindness and sharing reveal the depth of our relationship with him. Those who are growing to know Jesus will find themselves giving to others in the same way he gives to them. That is why at the end of the age he can measure our love for him by the love we gave to others: "For I was hungry and you gave me something to eat, I was thirsty and you gave me something to drink, I was a stranger and you invited me in,

I needed clothes and you clothed me, I was sick and you looked after me, I was in prison and you came to visit me" (Matt. 25:35–36). Those who didn't know Jesus questioned his words, asking when they saw him in need and didn't help. Jesus replied, "Whatever you did not do for one of the least of these, you did not do for me" (v. 45).

Our life in Jesus, or the lack of it, is demonstrated by our compassion for people in need. He looks at those actions exactly as if we are, or are not, doing them for him. His compassion is contagious. Once we have experienced it from his hand, there is no way we can hold it to ourselves.

## Discussion Questions

1. Describe a time when someone's kindness deeply touched you.
2. List some ways that you think God might be asking you to express his kindness to others.
3. Discuss the difficulties of being kind when you are angry or vengeful towards someone who wronged you.
4. How can you share with others in ways that do not involve money?
5. How do you react when Jesus says that when you do something for the least of people, you are doing it for him?

# Part 3

## sharing the journey

Having a friend to share your journey in uncertain moments and dark stretches will multiply your wisdom and courage greatly. We are not asked to go it alone but to enjoy the resources of others God has placed around us.

# 7

# lightening the load

**Serve one another.**

*Galatians 5:13*

**Carry each other's burdens.**

*Galatians 6:2*

**Build each other up.**

*1 Thessalonians 5:11*

I don't know what your destiny will be, but one thing I know: the only ones among you who will be really happy are those who will have sought and found how to serve.

Albert Schweitzer

Rick and Connie live in a coastal community near a navy base. One Saturday morning they noticed that the yard across the street needed some attention. The grass hadn't been mowed for a couple of weeks, and the weeds around the flowerbeds were taller than the plants. The house belonged to a navy couple, and the husband had been at sea for six months. He was due home the next day, and the wife had been so busy she had not yet gotten to the yard.

Connie had an idea.

"Rick," she said, "I'll pull the weeds if you'll mow the lawn."

After checking to make sure nobody was home, Rick and Connie mowed, weeded, and trimmed the plants, transforming the neglected yard. Without a note of explanation, Rick and Connie returned to their home and went about their day.

Early the next morning there was a knock on their door. It was their neighbor. "I knew it was you," Vickie said in tears when Rick opened the door. "I came home late last night thinking I would have to mow the lawn at midnight. When I saw my yard, I couldn't believe it. I just sat in the car for twenty minutes and cried. Thank you so much."

Where do Rick and Connie's actions fit in our one anothering passages? Serve one another? Carry each other's burdens? Build each other up? Maybe it should fall in the previous chapter—be kind to one another. How about all of them? Vickie didn't care about categories; all that mattered was that she got the help she desperately needed.

A week ago I was reminded of how valuable a gift lightening someone's load is as my wife and I were hiking in the Rockies up a steep trail to Hanging Lake outside Glenwood Springs, Colorado. It was a tough climb at that altitude on a hot day, and we stopped frequently to catch our breath. As we neared the top, however, we started to meet hikers who had gone before us and were now on their way down. Knowing how exhausted we were, they would look us in the eye and with a smile tell us, "It's worth it! Keep going! You're almost there."

Those who had already been up this trail knew the doubts and thoughts of giving up that we faced. Their words lightened our spirits, strengthened our resolve, and quickened our steps. Riding their enthusiasm, we made it to the top of the cliff and sat down to enjoy the fruit of our journey. It really had been worth it. On our way back down, we found ourselves speaking the same encouragement to those still on their way up. Knowing how much it had lightened our load, we wanted to share it with others.

The three one anothering Scriptures in this chapter show us how to help lighten someone else's load.

## "Serve One Another"

On the night before he was going to fulfill the ultimate act of service by giving his life for the world, Jesus was the only one willing to take up the towel and wash the dirty feet of his followers as they came into the upper room for the Passover meal. He never thought it beneath him to serve people in simple and practical ways. Love will cause us to put the needs of others above our own and to do so joyfully.

Finding ways to practically help others face the demands of life is a significant means of lightening their loads. That is what Rick and Connie did by sprucing up their neighbors' yard. When you live with others in mind, you too will find creative ways to help people around you.

Too often we see somebody in need and sincerely offer these words: "If there's anything I can do to help, don't hesitate to call." Well intentioned though it may be, usually the last thing on somebody's mind during a crisis is an organized list of what others can do. Their usual response is a thin smile and half-hearted thank you, but usually nothing gets done that lightens their burden. While most of us can't think of a practical thing to do when a family loses a loved one, a friend of mine has been known to go to the grieving family's house the day before the funeral and ask for all the shoes they will be wearing to the service. He takes them home and polishes each pair to perfection, then returns them that night so they are ready to wear the next day. E. W. Howe, early-twentieth-century American author and editor, said, "When a friend is in trouble, don't annoy him by asking if there is anything you can do. Think up something appropriate and do it."[1]

## Serving from a Heart of Love

Your week has been exhausting. Saturday rolls around, and between getting one child to her soccer game and the other to a birthday party, you desperately need to get some overdue bills in the mail. Then the phone rings, and someone from your fellowship tells you she needs you to take a dinner over to Mrs. Mitchell's house. You've never met Mrs. Mitchell, but her father passed away that morning. If you're anything like me, you feel compassion, but the first words out of your mouth are, "Is there anybody else you could call?"

Serving one another isn't always easy, nor is it fair to expect that we can meet every need that crosses our path. To attempt to do so would be an overwhelming burden. In Galatians 5, Paul points out that our freedom in Christ allows us to serve others with joy. The believers in Galatia were being told that they would have to follow the law in order to be acceptable to God. Paul doesn't pull any punches in condemning the errant teaching as a "yoke of slavery." Then in the midst of his great proclamation, he focuses their freedom on the joy of serving: "But do not use your freedom to indulge the sinful nature; rather, serve one another in love" (v. 13).

For Paul, service was not a weighty obligation but rather a natural result of walking in the Spirit. He concludes the passage by comparing our sinful nature with the fruit of the Spirit: love, joy, peace, patience, kindness, goodness, faithfulness, gentleness, and self-control. "Serving one another in love" marks the transition from being slaves to the law to living in the Spirit.

We marvel at Mother Teresa's incredible sacrifice, thinking we could never equal her care for the orphans of India. But what would you do if you drove up to your house one day and a six-year-old girl you knew and loved dearly was sitting on your sidewalk homeless and starving? Wouldn't it be easy to invite her into your home? Mother Teresa taught for twenty years in a convent school in Calcutta before she ever opened her orphanage. By allowing her heart to grow in love for those children, she reached out in the only way she knew to help. Service is the natural by-product of loving others.

So should we serve only those we know? Of course not! Though serving those we know will happen more naturally, an act of service may also start a new relationship—one that just might open a life to God's love. What's important is that we let love motivate us as the Spirit makes us aware of opportunities to serve. Serving out of obedience alone is slavery; serving with love is a joy.

Building relationships with others turns painful obligations into joyous service. Our service may not be as heroic as Mother Teresa's; it may be as simple as picking up a friend's kids from school, mowing the neighbor's lawn, or taking a meal to a family in need. As we keep our eyes open for the opportunities the Lord brings our way, we will know where we can serve others and do so in love.

## "Carry Each Other's Burdens"

Some things are just too awkward to carry alone. I have seen people try to muscle an awkward piece of furniture on their own. Usually they pull their back, ding the walls, or drop the load and damage it. As quickly as we would rush in to help someone carry a cumbersome load, we can help people carry even more difficult loads of inner struggle, hurt, or pain. This fallen world is full of ups and downs, trials and tribulations for everybody, and God does not intend for us to go through it alone.

On a men's retreat one weekend, Robert overheard someone ask his friend, Tim, if things had improved at work. Robert didn't know what needed improving, so he determined to find time that weekend to take his friend aside and ask. When Robert asked him, it took awhile, but Tim eventually began to open up. Things had gotten so bad at the company he had inherited from his father that he was sleeping only a couple of hours per night. He had postponed a family vacation and was miserable and fatigued.

Robert asked if he could pray for Tim. Right there in a shadowed corner by the basketball court, Robert put his hand on Tim's shoulder and shut his eyes. "But I couldn't pray," Robert told me. "A sudden flood of emotion came over me, and I began weeping. Every thirty seconds or so I could squeeze out a phrase of prayer, but then I had to stop just to hold the blubbering at bay. I went on like that for ten to fifteen minutes. I had no idea what was happening. All I knew was that God was allowing me to feel a hint of the crushing burden Tim was under."

Robert finally gave up and apologized to Tim while being unable to explain why he had been overcome. He learned later that the encounter had touched Tim tremendously. By getting under the load with Tim, Robert had helped to lift the load that weighed so heavily on his friend.

We don't have to find the "right words" or the "right prayer" to make a difference. When people go through difficult times, they rarely need someone who can fix their problem. Instead, they need someone who will walk with them through it.

Being more open about the burdens we labor under would be helpful. Tim had gone to that retreat determined to hold his need inside because he didn't want to ruin the weekend for anyone else. He almost missed getting the support he needed and giving Robert the joy of helping.

## "Build Each Other Up"

The final way we can lighten someone's load is not related to a practical need or even a specific challenge. Often Paul exhorted the early believers to build each other up, or as he also termed it, to edify one another. This act of love isn't designed to fix a specific problem but to nourish others in the life of Jesus. In fact, Paul saw edification as the prime objective when believers get together.

If we focus only on helping one another through the difficult moments, we soon will be consumed with problems and worn-out trying to address them all. Edifying one another is simply a way of putting our focus back on Jesus and the unfolding of life in us. It helps us grow closer to him and look beyond any current crisis to give attention to spiritual growth that will yield great rewards in days ahead.

A few years ago I met an Australian man whose ability to trust Jesus has impacted me deeply. Whenever I have been able to spend some time with him, which has been considerable in the years since, I always come away lighter in spirit, freer to trust Jesus myself. Just listening to him talk about Jesus or praying with him lifts me out of my own efforts to try harder and frees me to trust God more. I find myself less anxious for weeks afterward, less inclined to try to control everything around me, and far more confident in God's ability to work in me. I find myself quite naturally looking forward to every contact with this man. No wonder Paul said building up one another is at the heart of our church life.

Nourishing one another's spiritual life is simply serving spiritual food and drink to those who cross our paths. How can we do that? Whenever you get some time with another believer, look for ways to share what God is teaching you and doing in you. Share what you are learning about his nature that leaves you in awe of him. What have you been reading in Scripture that has spoken to your heart? How has he made his love known to you or known through you to someone else?

You often will find that as you share freely from your life, others will do the same. Hearing how others are learning to follow God and mining the wisdom they are uncovering from God's Word not only will enrich your own journey but will enhance the depth of fellowship you experience with others. This kind of sharing is the bread and butter of body life. By serving them up to others, you will help those people in ways you may not always notice at first but in ways that will bear fruit in them for years to come.

## Discussion Questions

1. Share a personal story of when a friend called at just the right time or came over to visit and built you up.
2. Compare a time when you felt pressured to serve out of obligation and when you did it out of relationship. How did you feel in each instance?

3. Sometimes it is harder to be served than to serve. Read John 13:1–17. How would you have felt if you had been one of the disciples that night?
4. Can you remember a time when someone helped bear a burden for you? How did he or she do it?
5. Brainstorm some creative ways you can help lighten one another's load in the next week.

# 8

# cheerleading

**Encourage one another daily.**

*Hebrews 3:13*

**Comfort one another.**

*1 Thessalonians 4:18 (NASB)*

**Stimulate one another to love and good deeds.**

*Hebrews 10:24 (NASB)*

There is nothing better than the encouragement of a good friend.

Katharine Butler Hathaway

I was on the verge of giving up. Though I thought I was doing what God wanted, circumstances seemed to prove otherwise. I was short on money, every plan I made had fallen apart, and I was afraid that my failure would only provide fuel to those who wanted to discredit me.

My whole vantage point, however, shifted with a phone call. A good friend of mine, on a business trip to Florida, called on the spur of the moment just to see how I was. I laid out my troubles and told him I was discouraged enough to quit. Gayle had been through a similar season and told me so. He ended by telling me one thing he had learned: "Don't forget: When you're following Jesus, time and light are on your side." He added that he believed in what I was doing and that I should just wait and see what God would do.

Hebrews 12:1 tells us that a great cloud of witnesses surrounds us. Because of their encouragement, we can lay aside everything that hinders or entangles us. When I read that passage, I see a cheering section filled with all the men and women of faith who have gone before us. They are cheering us on to follow Jesus no matter what the cost. But I don't seem to hear them when I need them most. For that I need a voice like Gayle's. His words gave me the courage to stay the course long enough to see God turn it around.

Encouraging one another, comforting one another, and stimulating one another to love and good deeds are three ways we cheer on believers around us. In the moments they most need it, find a way to whisper in their ear, "I believe in you!" "You're doing the right thing; stay with it!" "God is big enough to get you through this." The best way to know what to say is to look back at your own experience. What have people said to you that made it easier to trust Jesus, and what misguided words only made him seem farther away?

## "Encourage One Another Daily"

A long-term ministry relationship had soured, and the resulting ultimatum was clear. Forced to choose between the security of the fellowship I had served for fifteen years and staying true to my conscience, I found myself outside a group of people I dearly loved. I drove to the High Sierras to get out of town and sort out my conflicted feelings.

I stopped at my parents' house to drop off my things before my long walk in the woods. As I started for the door, my dad stopped me, saying, "I want to read you something before you go." In his hands was a copy of *The Message*, a paraphrase of the Bible by Eugene Peterson. He read: "Count yourselves blessed every time people put you down or throw you out or speak lies about you to discredit me. What it means is that the truth is too close for comfort and they are uncomfortable. You can be glad when that happens—give a cheer even!—for though they don't like it, *I* do. And all heaven applauds" (Matt. 5:11–12). Over the next few days that Scripture worked its way into my prayers and overturned my despair by allowing me to see my pain from God's perspective.

We encourage others by saying or doing things that make God more visible to them. The more we know of them, the more valuable our contribution can be. Of course, words of encouragement may be the most obvious means of encouraging others, but they are not necessarily the most powerful. Our mere presence, an I-was-just-thinking-about-you-today phone call, or a drop-by visit can offer great hope. A surprise gift or card can do the same thing.

In Paul's letters, encouragement is the language of church life, and the writer of Hebrews adds that we should do it "daily" (3:13). Anyone on a spiritual journey with Christ knows the way is often difficult, sometimes painful, and almost always filled with distractions. Being encouraged daily is not a luxury; it is a necessity. What encouragement we get from corporate gathering alone is not enough; we need further encouragement through personal relationships, and we would be well served if we would weave encouragement into the fabric of our lives and our interaction with others.

"Whom can I encourage today?" is a question we all can ask every day. When you know you are going to spend some time with someone, ask God what you might say or do that would help that person experience a touch of God's grace. Encouragement is not advice, platitudes, or empty words, like when someone says to the grieving, "Well, we know she's in a better place now." Godly encouragement says, "I know this must be really hard. Let me take care of the kids this afternoon. I'll be right here."

## "Comfort One Another"

Many readers may not think the word *comfort* fits our cheerleading theme. The image it brings to mind is someone with his or her arm around a troubled friend saying, "There, there! Everything will be okay."

But the word Paul uses in Thessalonians is a far richer word. It could be better translated as "to enable." In fact, this is the root word Jesus used as a name for the Holy Spirit. He called him "another Comforter" (John 14:16 KJV) who would come alongside and enable us to follow God's purpose.

Even Paul found himself in need of such comfort. At the beginning of his second letter to the Corinthians, he describes a horrible experience that he suffered with Timothy in Asia. "We were under great pressure, far beyond our ability to endure, so that we despaired even of life" (1:8). Can you imagine Paul and Timothy being so besieged that they didn't want to go on? Just knowing that men like Paul and Timothy had those feelings encourages me. Paul said that in the midst of their despair, God both comforted and delivered them. He looked back at their painful circumstances and concluded,

"This happened that we might not rely on ourselves but on God" (v. 9).

What comfort does best is get our eyes off our efforts and our limited resources and put them back on God and his power. That was the comfort that turned the tide for Paul and Timothy. Furthermore, Paul knew that the comfort they received was comfort they eventually could pass along to others. "If we are comforted, it is for your comfort, which produces in you patient endurance of the same sufferings we suffer" (2 Cor. 1:6).

That doesn't sound like mere commiseration with someone's pain, does it? This comfort enables people on the verge of giving up to set their eyes on God and see what he is doing in them. That is why Paul was the most prolific cheerleader of the first century. His letters are filled with the wonder of God's working and the depth of his love that will stand with us through anything.

## "Stimulate One Another to Love and Good Deeds"

Stimulating people to love and good deeds is not as simple as telling them what they should be doing. This latter often does more to discourage than it does to invite them into a greater revelation of God's grace. Though it can happen in a variety of ways, stimulating others to love and good deeds draws the best out of others by helping them see God's purpose in their lives.

My wife has a close friend who now lives hundreds of miles away. They may see each other once or twice a year. Recently my wife was under some heavy stress, and being the clueless husband, I hadn't taken notice. Fortunately, I can't recall the exact circumstances, but I do remember she was frustrated—at me! We had just taken our dogs for a walk around the block, a time when we often work through such things, but this time we remained distant.

When we returned, my wife decided to take a second loop—alone. I prayed that God would meet her there—well, actually I begged him—but the extra twenty minutes only increased her anger. She told me later that it was one of those times when she really enjoyed being mad and was looking forward to letting me have it when she got home.

As she came through the door, the phone rang. I answered it, and hearing the voice of her good friend, called to her that Tami was on the phone. She muttered to herself, knowing that Tami had a way of helping her see beyond the frustration of the moment. My wife actually picked up the phone laughing. I have thanked God many times for Tami.

My wife and Tami help each other reach for the best. My wife can share her frustrations—even while my ears are burning—and Tami knows how to help her see situations in a different light. My wife does the same for Tami. When either of them acts on the simple nudging of the Spirit to call the other, something wonderful usually results.

You can do the same for others. Your demeanor, thoughts, or simple affection can rescue people from their own anger, ego, or selfishness and free them to live on a higher plane in the life of Jesus.

## Kingdom Cheers

We can cheer one another in a variety of ways. Like Paul, we can honestly share those times we came to the end of our rope and found that God was doing even greater things than we could imagine. Paul wanted the Corinthians to know that there are times when believers can despair even of life, yet God can be bigger still. Often we will have greater compassion and insight for people struggling with the same things we have already been through. You will find those people drawn to you and you to them.

We also help people know God's heart for them when we remind them how Scripture speaks to their circumstances. My wife and I have often encouraged each other in our bleakest moments with the words of Jeremiah 29:11, "'For I know the plans I have for you,' declares the LORD, 'plans to prosper you and not to harm you, plans to give you hope and a future.'"

Another way to give encouragement is to tell people how much they have touched our lives. Unfortunately, many times those words go unspoken until someone dies. We need to bring our funeral talk into the land of the living. While I appreciate the incredible stories I hear at funerals, I am always saddened by the realization that the people we are memorializing probably never heard these things when they were alive. How much courage and strength it would have given them if they had only known.

Many small groups I have been a part of reserve an evening every few months and take turns focusing on one person at a time around the room. People are invited to share with the group what they see in that person's life that has blessed or encouraged them. Everyone leaves that room greatly encouraged to keep growing in Jesus.

You don't have to agree with everything a person believes or does to encourage him or her to draw closer to Jesus. Remember that when people are struggling, they are usually not in the mood to respond to criticism, even if it is constructive. We will talk later about speaking corrective words to one another, but when people are struggling, pointing them to Jesus will most help them grow closer to him. He will know how to make adjustments without increasing their pain.

## The Cheer That Doesn't Work

One of the most common statements people use to encourage one another is, "You just need to trust God more!" It rarely works. That is why Paul didn't use it. Most people who are told to trust God more in the midst of trouble and despair have to resist the urge to strangle the person telling them to do so. That's true for a couple of reasons. First, people offering that advice usually have no idea what trust is and freak out at the first sign of trouble in their own lives. Second, we cannot immediately trust God more than we already do. Trust is not something we can choose to increase on demand; it only grows as our security in God's love for us grows.

Telling someone to trust God reminds me of the father yelling at his third grader running in his first race. As Billy runs twenty-five yards behind the pack, his dad shouts, "Run faster, Billy; run faster!" Doesn't he think Billy has already thought of that and is giving it everything he has? Will increasing his embarrassment help? A good cheerleader for Billy might express pride that Billy tried so hard in his first race. He might offer to run with him after work every afternoon so he could work on his technique and conditioning. That is what cheerleading in this kingdom looks like.

When you come alongside people who have lost their job or are discouraged by sickness, think twice before telling them they just need to trust God more. Instead, you might tell them that God has not forgotten them, that God is bigger than their struggles and doubts, and that you will walk with them as they learn to lean on Jesus. Stimulating people to love and good deeds does not happen by picking at their failures or by pushing them to try harder; it happens by helping them draw closer to Jesus.

## Becoming More Like Jesus

When I moved back to the Los Angeles area after a show I directed in Nashville was canceled, I thought God had wanted to put me back into mainstream television production in Hollywood. But that first year, show after show that would boost my career passed me by. Even when producers raised my hopes during interviews, I'd hear later that they had picked another director.

I couldn't figure it out. I knew God had brought me back to Hollywood to be a light in the darkness. How could I be an influence if I wasn't working? Any career advancement I had would be his gain, wouldn't it? Yet others seemed to prosper, and I was left out. I remembered that David had felt the same way: "O LORD, how long will the wicked be jubilant? They pour out arrogant words; all the evildoers are full of boasting" (Ps. 94:3–4).

As my savings account dwindled and I lost another potential job that I thought suited me perfectly, I found myself spiraling into depression. Then on one gloomy morning—it was quite sunny outside, but my heart was overcast—I vented my frustration while playing golf with my brother. (There always seems to be enough money for a round of golf.) Walking up to the fifteenth hole, he gently responded with words that I will never forget: "God's priority for you may not be the best career path but the best way for God to make you more like Jesus."

It wasn't what I wanted to hear. Over the last few holes, however, it began to work its way into my heart, and I began to take my eyes off my agenda and to look to God's. Would I really want to have the "perfect" television job if it didn't help transform me more into the image of Christ?

If my brother had said something like, "You just need to trust God more," I might have taken a swing at him with my 9-iron. Instead of telling me to do what I wouldn't be able to do, he set my focus on God's working. As much as I wanted to believe him, one thing kept bothering me: What if I had made a mistake that made me miss what God wanted, either by moving back to California or by not doing well on the interview?

When I asked my brother about that, he smiled and set my fears at ease. "If God isn't bigger than our mistakes, then ultimately we're not trusting him; we're trusting our own performance. What kind of trust is that?" Take the time to read that again. Those are life-changing words.

The jobs didn't immediately come. But shortly after that round of golf, I sold a proposal for a new novel and had the time to complete the manuscript, something that would have been impossible if I had gotten the previous job. Even better than that, my eyes were no longer on my career frustrations but on God's purpose. He is faithful, and my trust in him grew as a result. It is ironic that as I write this chapter, the same show that I didn't get last year has hired me this fall. How wonderful it was to walk in God's peace before I saw his provision. If I had read further in Psalm 94, I would have seen how David, after venting his frustration, reminded himself of God's faithfulness: "For the LORD will not reject his people; he will never forsake his inheritance. . . . But the LORD has become my fortress, and my God the rock in whom I take refuge" (vv. 14, 22).

An old adage about writing fiction says, "Show, don't tell." The same is true in encouraging, comforting, and stimulating others. Don't tell them what they are doing wrong; don't tell them to try harder when they are doing their best—show them how to see God in the midst of their pain. Doing so will cheer them on, and it just might save you from a beating with a 9-iron.

## Discussion Questions

1. Think of times when you shared your frustration with other believers. What did they say that wasn't helpful? What did they say that helped you draw closer to Jesus?
2. Why do we tend to give pat answers (like "You just need to trust God more") to people in crises rather than sharing from our own experience?
3. Think of ways you can encourage one another daily. Don't create a program here, but think of ways you can be more aware of others and their need to be encouraged every day.
4. Share specific Scriptures that have spurred you along during times of discouragement.
5. Take the time to go around the room and share good things you see in one another's lives. How have those persons been used by God to touch your life?

# 9

# pooling our wisdom

**Instruct one another.**

*Romans 15:14*

**Admonish one another.**

*Colossians 3:16*

He who listens to a life-giving rebuke will be at home among the wise.

King Solomon
Proverbs 15:31

Isn't it interesting that you can spend all day wandering through the busy streets of Manhattan without anyone noticing you, yet anyone you pass on a hiking trail will not only notice you but usually will pause to find out where you have been and where you are headed? The street is anonymous—people passing in a hurry to get somewhere else. There are far too many people to even consider engaging in a conversation. You would never get anywhere. Loneliness flourishes in large crowds. But I have yet to pass anyone on a hiking trail who didn't stop and talk at least briefly. The camaraderie of the trails is immediate, even if you are not likely to see each other again. For those brief moments the help and insight two people share can make a huge difference.

If your Christian experience is a living journey instead of a plodding ritual, you will find the same thing to be true. When my Christianity was more static—consisting of attending services, doing church work, and trying to be good—my fellowship with others stayed shallow. I remember coming home many nights frustrated from having spent an entire evening with other people but somehow having been unable to move the conversation beyond the weather, sports, family, and current movies.

I wanted fellowship, but every time I would try to bring up something about God or Scripture, the conversation grew stilted and awkward. Only in the last few years have I come to recognize that Christianity is a journey into ever-deepening levels of relationship and ever-widening spaces of freedom. When you are on that journey, you will naturally talk about it in virtually every conversation you have, and when you connect with someone else who is sharing that journey, your conversation will be the best! Sharing the journey is as natural as breathing.

## Geese or Sparrows?

Watching a flock of Canada geese fly over in precise V-formation is an enthralling sight. How do you suppose they do that? Do they attend V-formation flying school when they are young? I can just see an older goose projecting a Powerpoint presentation against a birch tree and explaining to the younger birds how to fly two feet to the outside wing of the goose in front of them, one foot behind, and eighteen inches above its flight path so it will impress the humans below.

No, geese fly in a V-formation because flying in that exact spot allows them to fly in smoother air with less effort. If a goose falls out of position, it immediately feels the added stress of flying on its own and moves back into position. Scientists estimate that by drafting on the wake of the goose in front of them the entire flock is able to fly 71 percent farther than each of them could fly individually. To accomplish this incredible feat, the stronger birds in the flock will rotate the lead position so that no one bird wears out. According to NASA, "This allows a flock of birds with differing abilities to fly at a constant speed with a common endurance."[2]

The reason you never see a flock of sparrows fly in V-formation is because they are not going anywhere. They flit around the yard from tree to tree, but at the end of the day, they are in the same area. They could try to learn to fly in a V-formation, but by the time they got the formation together, they would already be to the next tree and not need it.

The same is true about fellowship. If Christianity is just about rituals, routines, and morals, our fellowship will suffer. We can rearrange our groupings or try a number of novel small-group techniques, but they will be as awkward as sparrows trying to fly in formation. But when Christianity is a life of growing dependence on God through the joys and challenges of our circumstances, pooling our wisdom becomes as natural an extension of that life for us as it is for geese to fly in formation. When God is more real to you than the weather and the events of your day, you will find him filling your conversations, and fellowship will be immediate, powerful, and alive.

## Journey Talk

I went to a men's breakfast group one morning where the participants pulled out scorecards and reported how many days the previous week they had read Scripture, witnessed to an unbeliever, or "hit their knees" before "hitting the shower." They were holding each other accountable to disciplines they thought important. As sincere as they may have been to encourage one another, they were sincerely wrong.

These men had embraced a process of conformity, thinking it was their responsibility to motivate people to comply with their standards. Little did they realize that this process is the opposite of sharing the Christian journey. That is why accountability groups start with a wealth of zeal and quickly fade away. Can you imagine Jesus pulling out similar scorecards to check on his disciples?

Growing in relationship with God does not come through conformity but through transformation. Relationships are organic and therefore defy all attempts to fit into any one-size-fits-all model. Rules, routines, and rituals are the building blocks of religion, not relationship. People caught up in religion focus on obeying authority, maintaining accountability, meeting standards by human effort, finding fault, confronting failure, and blaming others. In short, conforming to these things can be quite painful, especially for those who struggle to do the accepted thing. People instinctively know that instead of helping them know God better, these religious activities add stress and strain to the journey. That is why Paul told his readers over and over again not to have anything to do with people who wanted to boss others, even if their aim was greater righteousness (2 Cor. 11:13–15; Gal. 5:7–10, 6:11–19; Phil. 3:2; Col. 2:16–19).

Paul wasn't against righteousness, but he knew that true righteousness grew only out of a trusting relationship to the Father. This kingdom does not result from our efforts but from his. "Apart from me you can do nothing" (John 15:5), Jesus said, calling us to depend on him. We do not share the journey by conforming others to what we think is best for them, but by encouraging them to lean on Jesus.

Those on the journey talk about encouragement, help, service, support, love, compassion, forgiveness, and trust. They will focus on loving God more freely and one another more openly, trusting God instead of trusting themselves, being real instead of repeating "right" answers, and taking the risk to follow God instead of meeting people's expectations. They won't force people into a mold, because they know people have to have their own journey with God so he can transform them into his likeness. Doing so lifts people higher instead of weighing them down with added obligations and responsibilities.

## "Instruct One Another"

*Teach? Me? Absolutely not! I couldn't possibly do that. I hate standing in front of people.*

It is tragic that when most of us hear the word *teaching* we think of standing in front of a roomful of people lecturing. That is a small slice of what real teaching is. In fact, for most of human history, teaching was done one on one, in tutoring or apprenticeships. When you share a favorite recipe with a friend; tell someone about a favorite article, book, or thought; or show a child how to use a fork, you are teaching.

We all are teachers. Sharing with others the insights God drops into our lives or lessons we have picked up from others is the most powerful process for learning the lessons we need for the journey. The vast majority of teaching doesn't happen in lecture halls, but in conversations in which we share what we have discovered to help others.

One of the hardest things to motivate small group participants to do is to come ready to share. We have for so long been schooled in the notion that we gather as a body to receive what a few professionals have prepared for us that believers shy away from sharing a song, a word, a prayer—anything! Getting together with other Christians should be like a spiritual potluck in which everyone brings something different to share (1 Cor. 14:26).

I once met with a home group that grew awkwardly quiet as we began. It was the kind of meeting everyone dreads, because no one has anything to share. After a song or two, it was clear that we weren't going anywhere. "It seems to me that we're all a bit tired tonight," I ventured. People nodded. "Did anyone bring anything to share with us?" Everyone looked around the room, but there were no takers. "We have two choices, then. We can either press through our tiredness and see if God has something for us tonight, or we can just admit that we're all tired and unprepared, call it a night, and try again next week."

We agreed to try again next week. It was only a ten-minute meeting but a powerful learning experience. We didn't force anything to happen, nor did we go through the motions just to make ourselves feel good. If we had, it would have been the same as pretending to eat at a potluck to which no one had brought food. We wouldn't do it, nor would we ask our hosts to empty their freezer and feed everyone who hadn't come prepared.

Until that notion of body life captures our heart and we realize that God wants to use each of us to share his wisdom with others, we will miss out on the best teaching available in the body of Christ today. Whenever I see something in Scripture that touches my life, I always look for someone else it might bless.

## "Admonish One Another"

"Don't you think that was the most manipulative thing you've ever said?"

I couldn't have been more shocked at my friend's words. He always encouraged me in things I had written or preached, and I thought yesterday's sermon on having a heart for outreach had been one of my best. I had looked forward to our lunch appointment all day, because I knew Dave would be impressed.

"You're kidding, right?" I said, laughing it off. His face told me he wasn't. I told him how powerful I thought the message had been and about the positive feedback others had given me.

"I could be wrong," he said shrugging his shoulders, "but it looked to me like you were manipulating people with guilt to make them do what you wanted. I've learned that any time my success depends on another person's response, I will manipulate them."

Only after a few days of mulling over my friend's words in prayer did I finally understand. Even though my aim was noble, I had manipulated my audience, and I called Dave to tell him so. That one conversation changed my life in powerful ways. Dave had spoken the truth to me out of a personal friendship that allowed it to bear fruit.

I love the way Dave spoke to me. He had the relationship to speak truthfully and firmly to me—as my friend, not my judge. He was honest with me but didn't try to convince me even when I resisted. He trusted that God would have to make it clear. That is admonishment—our willingness to be gently honest with people we see making hurtful choices.

How many times have you walked away from a conversation wishing you had been more honest?

Admonishment was part of the early church's body life. Paul rebuked Peter for discriminating against Gentile believers in the face of his Jewish friends (Gal. 2:11–15). And the writer of Hebrews rebuked believers who were throwing away their confidence in difficult times (Heb. 10:35–39). Still, the New Testament uses words like *encourage* or *build up* fifty-six times and *rebuke* or *admonish* only seven times. That seems like a pretty good ratio to me. Though I have learned some of my greatest lessons from Dave, he has affirmed God's work in me at least eight times more than he has pointed out something that concerned him.

When people use admonishment to point out the faults of others so the former feel better about themselves, they kill genuine fellowship. We are not called to confront one another constantly or hold one another to exacting standards. We are to encourage one another along the journey of being transformed by God and only admonish others when it will help them walk in greater wisdom.

Our past encouragements will make any admonishment easier to heed. Don't force admonishment on others. Share what you see, and trust the Holy Spirit to make it clear to them. Remember, we are only sharing a journey; we are not called to badger one another into righteousness or nitpick at one another's faults.

## Discussion Questions

1. What experiences have you had in the past with other believers that made your journey easier? Which made it more difficult?

2. Explore some ways your group could share what you are learning with one another, both at group times and in personal conversations.
3. What is God teaching you in your personal life?
4. Can you think of some times when people have admonished you and it was helpful? What about times it wasn't so helpful? What made the difference?

# 10

# taking it to god

**Pray for one another.**

*James 5:16*

To pray "in Jesus' name" means to pray in his spirit, in his compassion, in his love, in his outrage, in his concern. In other words, it means to pray a prayer that Jesus himself might pray.

Kenneth L. Wilson

I'm not sure I can pray that way for you."

You would have thought I'd just cussed by the way the mouths around the table soundlessly fell open. The woman who had just asked us to pray that God would keep her teenage daughter from moving in with her boyfriend was perhaps the most shocked of all. Our home group had just finished dinner and was sharing about the past week. With obvious distress, Jill had told of her daughter's plan.

Once they all caught their breath, I explained. "I think all of us here can understand why you want God to stop her from doing that, but if we pray that way, aren't we asking God to violate her will?"

I could see Jill was about to lose it in frustration or anger, so I hurried on. "What I'd like to pray is that God would reveal himself to your daughter and let her see clearly the choice she is making. And I also want to pray for you—that God will show you how to trust him and how to love your daughter even if she makes the stupidest mistake of her young life."

I had hardly finished when Jill blurted out through her tears, "That's exactly what I need."

One of the best ways to share the journey is to take our concerns to God together, helping one another tap into his wisdom and power. As with the other aspects of one anothering, we will see again in this section that the better we get to know someone, the more effective we can be in loving them. Our knowledge of others and our compassion for them are powerful tools in prayer.

Have you ever been asked to pray for someone you didn't know? Those prayers are often generalized and lacking significant empathy. How would you pray for someone you don't know who has breast cancer? Wouldn't it be very different if the victim were your friend Kathy, who is raising her two children, ages four and seven, alone ever since her husband abandoned them two years before, and who is struggling financially with no health insurance?

## Praying for Others as Jesus Would

All that has been written on prayer through the ages—from the earliest prayers of Moses all the way to the prayers of believers of our day—could fill libraries. How can we take all of that information and learn to pray in the context of "one anothering"—praying together in ways that will encourage, uplift, and serve others along their journey in Christ?

The quote that heads this chapter embodies many of those aspects—praying with Jesus' compassion and love, even with his outrage at what the enemy is trying to accomplish, and always with his concern. That's the kind of prayer I want to pray for those around me. But to do that, I need to be in tune with the Lord's purpose in people. Too often I listen to prayer requests and then jump in and pray however I am asked. Is that the best way to do it?

Let's take an exaggerated example to make the point. Suppose a woman approached you and said, "Please pray for me. I've decided to leave my husband for another man, and I want God's peace about it." Would you be willing to pray that way for her? Of course not, but this case is obvious; other requests outside God's purpose may not be so apparent. In Jill's situation it would seem appropriate at first glance to pray that her daughter would not move in with her boyfriend. That was the desire of all us in the home group, but was it the right way to pray? Should we expect God to supersede the daughter's free will when we know that is not his nature?

But what could possibly be more important than Jill's daughter making such a huge mistake? I can think of two things—that she would come to a relationship with Jesus and that Jill herself would be able to trust God and show love to her daughter no matter what her decision.

When someone asks me to pray for a need in his or her life, the actual request is not where I begin. My first step is to ask God how he would have me pray. Now I know you are thinking, *I have a hard enough time finding God's will for my own life; how am I going to find it for someone else?* That is a valid question, but I'm not saying you are responsible for finding the will of God for others, just that it would be better to take the time to ask God to reveal how you should pray. Then pause to listen and see how the Spirit prompts you. It very well could be exactly what they requested, or it could be something quite a bit different. In either case, my desire is to pray as close to what God would want as possible. Could that be what it means to pray by the Spirit? Imagine how much confidence we will have in prayer when we know we are in harmony with God's will.

## Don't Hold Back

With all the great reasons for furthering our relationships through prayer, too often praying for someone on the spot feels awkward. There may be a lot of reasons for that, but the one I hear most often is that people are intimidated to pray in front of others.

We have the mistaken notion that God values eloquence over compassion and that he will hear us only if we can find just the right words. Prayer isn't a performance; it is an honest expression of our hearts to God. You will find yourself more effective if you can relax and be real before God with your concerns, desires, and requests.

Picture talking to God like a five-year-old crawling into her daddy's lap and sharing with him her hurts, frustrations, wants, and needs. It doesn't matter if she makes a mistake or is unsure of what to say; he already knows her heart and is thrilled to have the moment with her. Share honestly what is on your heart with your heavenly Father. Jesus' work allows us to do that. Often the less-than-perfect prayer can minister more to the one you are praying for than a perfect oration from a pulpit. We can come as we are, with all of our imperfections, and the God of the universe is not only there to listen but to show us his desires and share an intimate friendship.

Sharing a moment of prayer with another believer over a concern of theirs or yours can turn the tide and open doors to God's working. That is why Jesus reminded us that where two or three come together in his name, he will be right there with them (Matt. 18:20). When people ask you to keep them in prayer, don't just promise to add them to your prayer list. Ask them if you can draw away to an inconspicuous place right then and spend a few moments praying. You won't have to worry about forgetting, and you will find the experience far more powerful than doing it alone later.

## Suggestions for Praying Effectively

*Pray in small teams or one on one.* Praying in small groups gives us time to process someone's struggle and help identify God's work. Even home-sized groups can be too big for this kind of prayer. I have always found it more effective to break down into groups of two or three and give participants time to explore the situation together.

*Relate the situation, not just your request.* If we ask for a very specific result in our prayer request, we drastically limit the way others can pray. I once had a friend ask our group to pray that his brother who was in the military would not be sent to the Gulf War when his unit was scheduled for deployment. That made people feel limited in how they could pray. Wouldn't it have been more effective if he had told us of his brother's circumstances and his fears for his safety? Then we could have prayed not only for his safety but also for his attitude, his dependence on the Lord, and a variety of other possibilities. It would even allow for us to pray for his fear and ability to trust God through the situation.

*Look at the situation from God's perspective.* Before jumping in to request what you want, pause and think about what God might want. Most of our prayer requests fit what we think is best and may run counter to what God wants. I love how Peter and John responded to the Pharisees' threats that they stop sharing about Jesus or face severe punishment (Acts 4:15–31). Certainly they were frightened, but when they gathered later with other believers to pray, they didn't ask for what would be easiest for them. They could have prayed that God would convert the Pharisees the next day or wipe them from the face of the earth. But they didn't see either of those options as fitting God's work in history nor Jesus' example. Instead, they prayed for boldness to continue to do what God asked even when they knew they might well be beaten, imprisoned, or executed for it.

One of the things I most appreciate about Henry Blackaby's *Experiencing God* curriculum is that it invites us to trust that God can show us what he is doing in each situation. Sadly, too many people see prayer as our way to shape God instead of his way to shape us.

*Let your prayers flow from trust.* Fear is the death of prayer, because it is the opposite of trust. Most of my prayers even into my early forties were driven by my anxieties and fears. I have realized something in this process: The best measure of my relationship with Jesus is my ability to trust him no matter what circumstance I'm in. He rarely answered those prayers that asked him to fix my circumstances so that I could trust him less. His desire has always been that I would trust him more. Prayers that arise out of our security in his love and our confidence in his nature will be the most effective. So when I realize that I'm coming to God from a place of insecurity or fear, I first pray for a fuller revelation of God's love for me in the midst of my circumstance. That puts me in a better position to seek his will and trust the outcome to be what is best for me from an eternal perspective.

*Don't assess blame.* It is easy to fall into a trap and think God will answer our prayers if we are just good enough.

When we think that way, it is easy to blame the person in need when the answer we expect doesn't come. I watched my brother succumb to multiple sclerosis and pass away just three days shy of his forty-ninth birthday. We had prayed for him consistently over the twelve years he battled the disease. Convinced that God's only desire would be to heal him, we were frustrated when his MS worsened. Thinking there must be something he was doing wrong to keep God from healing him, we started probing weaknesses in his life. What a horrible thing for anyone, much less someone suffering through such hardship, to endure that kind of scrutiny!

Blaming people for unanswered prayer puts the focus on the person instead of on God. It's a normal reaction. When I took flying lessons as a young man, I was amazed at how often pilots speculated pilot error was to blame whenever they heard about a plane crash. It wasn't that they hated their fellow pilots; it was that all of them wanted to believe that if they did everything the way it was supposed to be done, they would be crash-proof. Many believers feel the same way. We don't like to think that catastrophic things can happen to devout believers. But they do, and instead of allowing us to support one another in times of crisis, such thinking distances us from others at the time they need us most.

I don't know why God didn't heal my brother, and I probably won't have the answer until I see him again in heaven—but it doesn't mean that because he wasn't healed it was somehow his fault. Unfortunately, we live in a fallen world, and all of us have to deal with disease and death. It also doesn't mean that my prayers for him to be healed were somehow a waste of time. We can be faithful in our love even if it appears the prayer has not been answered in the way we desired. Continuing to be diligent is when prayer crosses over into other areas of one anothering—loving, uplifting, bearing burdens, serving, and encouraging.

*Pray in unity.* Whenever you pray with people, don't be afraid to discuss with them what is on your heart and see if it sounds right to them. If they agree, you can pray together in unity. If not, don't try to coerce them. If what was on your heart came from God, the seed has been planted. They might come back at another time and ask you to pray in that direction then. Your discussion might uncover some areas where you really do agree. I find great encouragement when two or three people looking at the same situation from different angles share a common insight into God's working. When two of us agree, Jesus said, his Father in heaven will do what we ask for (Matt. 18:19).

*Praying Scripture.* Borrowing prayers from Scripture will help you pray for others knowing that your prayers are in the will of God. Look at the way Paul prayed:

- I pray . . . that the eyes of your heart will be enlightened. (Eph. 1:18)
- I pray that out of his glorious riches he may strengthen you with power through his Spirit. (Eph. 3:16)
- We pray this in order that you may live a life worthy of the Lord and may please him in every way. (Col. 1:10)
- We constantly pray for you . . . that by his power he may fulfill every good purpose of yours and every act prompted by your faith. (2 Thess. 1:11)

Other Scriptures can help us tune into God's heart for people in the midst of struggle as we pray for them:

- But those who hope in the LORD<br>        will renew their strength.<br>They will soar on wings like eagles;<br>        they will run and not grow weary,<br>        they will walk and not be faint. (Isa. 40:31)

- Cast your cares on the LORD
 and he will sustain you;
 he will never let the righteous fall. (Ps. 55:22)
- Because of the LORD's great love we are not consumed,
 for his compassions never fail.
 They are new every morning;
 great is your faithfulness. (Lam. 3:22–23)

*Follow up.* Nothing expresses our concern for those in need more than following up with a phone call a few days after we have prayed with them to see how they are doing and what happened as a result of our prayers. I'm convinced we don't often do follow-up because we have so little hope that our prayers will affect much and don't like to be reminded. But if the goal is to zero in on what God is doing and see him accomplish his will in our circumstances, then our initial prayer only begins the process.

If nothing has happened, we can ask God for wisdom. Is he doing something else in this situation other than we thought? Is he teaching us to persevere in what we started? Staying in the process until something is resolved will not only be a blessing but will train us for future opportunities in prayer.

The other benefit to following up with the people we pray for is that it gives us a chance to rejoice with them as we see how God is moving in the situation. It often helps to have a separate pair of eyes along our journey to point out where the Lord is walking beside us.

Philippians 4:6 invites us to make any request we want of God, but it does not tell us to expect him to answer the way we want. Scripture and life experience make clear that he is not a fairy godmother who will wave a magic wand and conform every circumstance to our whim. Real prayer is the process of getting involved with someone's need, praying as best we understand God's work, and then staying in the situation until we see his work resolved. Learning to do that well can lead to effective prayers and wonderful growth in our relationships.

## Discussion Questions

1. Can you think of a prayer request God didn't answer the way you wanted, but which turned out far better than what you thought?
2. Discuss what your reaction would be if somebody felt led to pray in a different direction than your original request.
3. What keeps you from praying at the spur of the moment for those who ask?
4. Think of ways we can make our prayers more like those that Jesus would pray.
5. Read the story of Peter and John's prayer when they were threatened by the Jewish religious rulers (Acts 4:23–31). What can we learn from this example of praying through adversity?

# Part 4

## for mature relationships

As you share your journey with others, you will find that some of those relationships will deepen as others demonstrate their love and concern for you. When you discover relationships like that, you are on the brink of enjoying the deepest expressions of one anothering.

# 11

# the genuine article

**Confess your sins to one another.**

*James 5:16 (NASB)*

**Be of the same mind toward one another.**

*Romans 12:16 (NASB)*

Our churches are filled with people who outwardly look contented and at peace, but inwardly are crying out for someone to love them . . . just as they are—confused, frustrated, frightened, guilty, and often unable to communicate with their own families. But other people in the church look so happy and contented that one seldom has the courage to admit his own deep needs before such a self-sufficient group as the average church meeting appears to be.

Keith Miller

Rachel seemed like the ideal Proverbs 31 woman. As a wife and mother, she juggled a vast array of responsibilities and always came out on top. Her home and yard were immaculate and her children well behaved. She volunteered for ministry and served responsibly in every task she accepted. Her life was the envy of many. Anyone who knew her would have been shocked by her revelation that morning. Her eyes filling with tears, she confessed to me that she was overwhelmed with loneliness. She said no one seemed to care about her. Everyone took advantage of her gifts, but for all the people who had flowed through her life, no one had become a close friend and confidant.

What began as a diatribe against the unfriendliness of our fellowship soon became a moment of self-discovery. As we talked, Rachel began to recognize that others held her at arm's length because they wrongfully assumed that she was above them. What could they possibly add to her flawless life? Rachel realized that morning that she was so busy sustaining an illusion of the perfect wife, mother, and believer that no one could get to know her.

"Have you ever shared this part of yourself with anyone?" I asked her.

"Not before today," she answered. "It's too embarrassing."

But that is exactly where she needed to start. Relationships are not built on illusions; they are built on the real struggles of life. Like Rachel, many of us spend so much time projecting the perfect Christian image that others never get the chance to know who we really are. We blame others for not caring when we haven't given them anything real to care about. What endears people to one another is the reality of their struggles, doubts, and weaknesses. Without that honesty our relationships will remain shallow.

## The Power of Confession

We don't confess our sins to one another as a condition for God's forgiveness. Rather, we confess our sins because Jesus' work on the cross has already secured our forgiveness.

Scripture encourages us to confess our sins to one another so that we can invite others into our struggles.

Aren't your closest friends those who know the most about you yet love you anyway? When you are around them, you feel no compulsion to pretend, and you find yourself living authentically in their presence. Unfortunately, too few people ever experience relationships at that level.

"I know no one else struggles with this, but . . ." I have heard dozens of people use that line as they begin to expose some area of their life that they have kept hidden. In reality we all are struggling. There is no temptation, weakness, or doubt that does not also cause others to struggle. The fact that people don't know that underscores the lack of genuine friendships among believers. Our fear of letting people see beyond the image we want to project denies us the friendships for which we hunger.

The freedom to confess our sins, expose our doubts, and let people see into our struggles accomplishes three things. First, it allows others to know us as we really are, which helps cultivate relationships. Second, it allows us to seek forgiveness from the people our failures and weaknesses have wronged and look for ways to make restitution. Finally, it allows God's light to shine on our brokenness and others to come to our aid, which greatly enhances the healing process.

## As Relationships Mature

The reason I saved confession and submission as the last two one anothering Scriptures is because they grow in expression as relationships mature. We don't open up the darkest places in our lives and submit our choices to strangers or new acquaintances; this happens naturally as friendships deepen. Being honest with people isn't easy, because most of us have been abused or manipulated by others precisely at our weakest points. We do not need to be open with others just because they call themselves believers, but we can allow relationships to grow so that people can appropriately handle the depth of our sharing.

A few years ago my wife and I moved to a new city where we knew absolutely no one. We had heard about a home group in that city that was intentionally looking to touch those in their early twenties and were excited to find out more. We visited one night, hopeful of finding believers who were actively engaged in the art of one anothering.

We were quickly disappointed. One of the first things they did was pass out three laminated pages to three different people in the room. Each read in turn their "rules of fellowship" that sought to ensure each of us that we would be treated with respect, love, and confidentiality.

Although I applaud their desire to create an environment where people feel free to be honest, I fault their methods. Their "rules" could only provide a substitute for the intimacy borne of real relationship. In the long run, they were only providing an illusion of intimacy rather than intimacy itself. One thing I have learned over the years is that anyone who is prone to gossip about you is also willing to lie about it. There is no substitute for real relationships that grow over time. Relationships are an organic reality, and it will not take you long to figure out which people around you are safe to open up to and which are best given a wide berth. Even among those who claim to be part of the church, you will find many who are persistently critical, self-centered, and destructive. They gossip, twist your words, and spare no effort to force their opinions on you. While we can still love those who are held captive by such deeds, we do not have to give them access to the depths of our hearts.

As you learn to freely love people around you, you will find scattered throughout those relationships people who demonstrate the same love and care for you. Through your contact with them, you will discover that they are a safe place to unpack some of your baggage, and you will find yourself journeying with them to ever-deepening levels of authenticity.

## The Measure of Fellowship

In my travels I often am asked how I assess the health of a particular group. I know people are looking for affirmation that they are doing things right, but I don't consider it my place to give them an evaluation. Instead, I give them a measuring stick: Compare the amount of gossip that goes on in the group with the amount of confession. The two can't exist side by side. You won't find people's weaknesses being whispered about in corners when they are not trying to hide them. Sin always thrives in the shadows, and where people are learning the freedom of authenticity, there are fewer shadows in which to hide.

Those who hide their own weaknesses, however, will make sport of highlighting the weaknesses of others. Such easy sport it is too! Since we all are in the process of being transformed, seeing one another's faults isn't difficult. Those who gossip only do so because they are frustrated by their own failures and only feel good about themselves when tearing down others. They exaggerate people's weaknesses and make assumptions about their motives. These tactics destroy fellowship and splinter groups. Each side goes away feeling superior to the other, never realizing that their perceptions of each other are often based on their own imaginations.

Where fellowship exists, real gossip has no place. It is easily exposed by honest questions and stopped in its tracks when people are unwilling to further rumors. Whenever someone complains to me about something someone else has said or done, I stop him or her before the luscious details, even when I am tempted to hear them. I say something like, "Before you go any further, let me call that person over or arrange a lunch together so we can all sort it out." You won't believe how quickly that stops gossip.

Wouldn't you love to live among a group of people where nothing harmful is shared about another person outside his or her hearing, where honesty is so prevalent that there is no room to hide in the darkness? That is what John meant when he wrote about walking in the light (1 John 1:5–10; 2:9–11). He didn't mean we would walk in perfection, but that we would walk in the freedom of sincerity so that we could be known for who we are and engage the process of transformation.

## The Freedom of Authenticity

One day those who paid my salary demanded that I follow their desires even when I told them that doing so would defy my conscience. Making the decision to separate from them was one of the hardest things I have ever done. I wasn't sure I was right and they were wrong. I knew I could be blinded by my own ambition and certainly did not want to make that mistake.

Eventually, however, I knew I couldn't stay. I didn't reach that decision by concluding that I was smarter or more spiritual than them. What freed me to do it was the desire to be known for who I really was. If my departure was an act of independent selfishness, I needed to know that. If it was the leading of God, I needed to know that as well. I remember praying, "Father, this is the best decision I know to make. Let it be seen for what it really is. If I'm wrong, let everyone know. If I'm following you, please confirm it." Only when I was willing to live in the truth, however it sorted out, was I free to do what I thought God wanted.

It wasn't easy. I had been pretending most of my life. I was always good at figuring out what others expected and meeting their expectations. That had gotten me through college and twenty years of vocational ministry. I was wired to other people's approval and was devastated whenever anyone didn't like something I said or did. Even in the midst of this decision, my colleagues in ministry appealed to this desire, asking, "What will others think?"

Finding freedom from the tyranny of other people's opinions is one of the greatest joys of life in Jesus. As long as you live for other people's approval, you are owned by anyone who chooses to lie about you. We are to liberate people from the desire for approval rather than exploit it to get them to "act more Christian." Jesus did not come to train a generation of actors but to transform people to live authentically in the world.

I love John Stott's definition of humility. In an interview with *Christianity Today* commemorating his eightieth birthday, this well-known English author and theologian said that humility is "not another word for hypocrisy; it is another word for honesty. It is not pretending to be other than we are, but acknowledging the truth about what we are."[3]

Living authentically is the freedom to be known exactly as we are—strengths and weaknesses rolled into one. People who understand God's heart love this way of life, while others less enlightened will expend their efforts trying to appear better than they really are.

## Manipulation-Proof

Living authentically will free you of other people's attempts to manipulate you. Trying to "act Christian" will often lead you into no-win situations, and being nice to those who manipulate will only draw you deeper into their web.

"I couldn't believe the gall of that man," a woman said to me with rising anger in her voice. She pointed to the chair next to mine. "He sat right in that chair reading his Bible while I cooked him breakfast every morning, and then he went out and lied about my husband to everyone else in our fellowship."

The man she spoke of had long since left that home and fellowship, but not before damaging many relationships and the hospitable heart of that woman. He had abused her hospitality and exploited her generosity. I would have thrown him out on his rear end the first morning he hadn't offered to help with the breakfast he was about to eat. I certainly wouldn't have been silent in the face of his deceit.

Authenticity will not allow us to stay silent in the face of exploitation. How many times have we walked away from situations wishing we had had the courage to say what we were really thinking rather than smiling pleasantly and pretending we agreed? That is part of confession too. We may not always get it right and will undoubtedly make mistakes, but we do not have to allow ourselves to be anyone else's victim. Even when I speak when I shouldn't or am insensitive to someone else's need, authenticity allows me to go back, apologize for my errors, and offer restitution wherever appropriate.

I'm sure you, like me, have seen people who are rude and obnoxious in the name of "being real." That is not what I'm talking about here. Any of the one anothering Scriptures can be abused to justify the most absurd behaviors. But authenticity is never an excuse to be rude or condescending to others. While we are free to speak truthfully, we are admonished to do so with the love and tenderness of Jesus Christ.

## A Confessional Climate

How do we create a climate in which people can be authentic? Don't suppose that you can ask a group to share their darkest sins as a stepping-stone to being confessional. Actually, in such moments people will only pretend to be authentic, and that will be even worse. A confessional climate cannot be created by artificial means. The best way to encourage a confessional climate is to model an authentic lifestyle yourself. As with all the other principles in this book, it begins in you before it can be expressed outside of you. You will be authentic with others to the degree that you are honest with yourself, and you will be honest with yourself to the degree that you will open your whole life to Jesus.

Do you remember the account of the immoral woman who approached Jesus in the home of a Pharisee to pour perfume over his feet and dry them with her hair (see Matt. 26:6–13)? How could that woman walk into a room where every person except one held her in contempt? She could do so because the only one who didn't despise her was the only one who mattered. Jesus had touched her life and forgiven her; what anyone else thought was irrelevant.

Likewise, when we are honest on the inside, we will find ourselves quite naturally authentic with others. Even though the depth of confession will grow as relationships do, we will not just be authentic with people we know well. Jesus will free us to be genuine in every situation. We will never again feel the need to project an image or pretend agreement when it really isn't in our heart.

That doesn't mean we will bring every person into the depths of our struggles. If at any time in your life you have three to four people with whom you can share your deepest temptations and struggles, you are indeed a blessed person. This kind of confession doesn't need to happen in gatherings of the body. It will more likely take place in relationships that have been spawned by those gatherings. Express yourself only to a Christian brother or sister who you know will treat your confession as God would—who will listen with compassion, help you see the truth about your sin so you can live forgiven and free as well, and stand with you in the struggle to walk in Christ's freedom. People who are being transformed by God's love are the safest place to fall. They are the people you want to catch you in your worst moments. They will understand your struggle and love you in it even as they will lend a hand to help you walk out of it into God's truth with God's power.

If you have found such people, you have found great treasure. But don't stop there. Ask Jesus to transform you so you can free others to live in the light instead of having to hide in the darkness.

## Discussion Questions

1. Tell about an incident in which being nice conflicted with being honest. What did you do? In hindsight, what do you wish you had said or done?
2. How does the thirst for other people's approval diminish who Jesus wants us to be? Read Galatians 1:10.
3. As you look around the room, to what degree do you think people are free to be genuine? What would help enlarge that freedom?
4. What needs to happen in you to free you to live a more authentic life?

# 12

# partnering in the journey

**Submit to one another.**

*Ephesians 5:21*

[Submission] is the ability to lay down the terrible burden of always needing to get your own way.

Richard Foster

"What do we do now?" John's voice sounded tormented. "We listened to everything said last night and have prayed and talked all day, and we still feel like we're supposed to go."

John and Marcy desired to go overseas with Youth With A Mission for discipleship training and outreach on a mercy ship. They wanted to submit their plans to a group of believing friends for direction, so we had met the night before to pray with them and discuss the pros and cons of their opportunity. In the end, everyone in that room except John and Marcy felt this was not the time for them to go.

John had just returned to their marriage a few weeks earlier after having left Marcy a year before on the day their third child was born. He had been overwhelmed by the responsibility and, desiring more freedom, had abandoned his young family. We felt it was too early for them to launch out on a ministry expedition when John needed to reconnect with his family first.

Despite our serious concerns, John and Marcy were too excited to be dissuaded. While they listened carefully and wrestled with our concerns, they still felt God wanted them to go. We asked them to give it another twenty-four hours to see what God might show them.

Now John was on the phone. Should he and Marcy yield to the group's wisdom or follow what they honestly believed God had put in their heart? I encouraged them to follow their heart. Submission in the body of Christ does not reduce decision-making to majority rule.

Even though we didn't end up in agreement, John and Marcy modeled true submission. They had arrayed their choices and motives before others. They had discussed them, prayed about them, and even given weight to what others thought. They still felt drawn to go, however, and we freed them to do it. To further demonstrate the power of this kind of submission, when John and Marcy left, some of their largest financial contributions came from the people in that room. Amazing? No! That's submission! It allows us to partner with others in the process of being changed by Jesus, not to control them to do what we think best.

Did John and Marcy make the right choice? They called a few months later, convinced that they had made a mistake in going, and it had cost them dearly. Then they asked, "Now that we've made a mistake, should we come home?"

They agreed to put that question before God in prayer, and I agreed to call some of the people who had been there that night to see what they thought. In the end, everyone felt that they should stay and that God would use even this mistake to further his will. Twenty years later, John and Marcy are still working in missions and have borne tremendous fruit for God's kingdom.

## Loving Not Conforming

Submission allows us the joy of partnering with others in the journey. It lets us share our insights without controlling one another's actions. Unfortunately, however, more abuse travels through the body of Christ under the guise of submission than any other admonition, often making believers a battered group of individualists rather than people who can effectively help others.

Some church leaders mistakenly teach that submission demands that believers capitulate to their leadership. Since institutions need conformity to survive, the demand for submission is an easy tool for keeping people in line. Throughout church history, people's submission to Jesus Christ has been questioned if they disagreed with the established leadership of the day.

Whenever institutional needs conflict with relational priorities, it is usually the relationships that suffer. That is why relationships among many Christian groups can be so fickle. If someone asks the wrong question or points out a problem others want to ignore, an individual can move from being a wonderful gift one moment to a dangerous rebel the next.

If the church is going to demonstrate the love of Christ in this generation, we are going to have to find a way to make institutional needs a distant second to healthy and supportive relationships. I know many people who already live that way. The godliest people I know don't jump into the power plays that dominate congregational battles; instead, they step aside, seeing institutional power as insignificant in comparison with God's larger purpose. They know submission is not a power game. It never asks anyone to subordinate his or her will to another. While Hebrews 13:17 tells us to yield to those in leadership, Paul uses an entirely different word when he invites believers to the joy of mutual submission. Leaders who demand that others submit to them are usually asking for unquestioned obedience, and ultimately it is always destructive. Submission at the hands of those bent on using others to fulfill their agenda is like a kitchen knife in the hands of a four-year-old—a powerful tool becomes a terrifying danger.

One evening I joined two elders who wanted me to meet with them and a woman in our fellowship who had recently separated from her husband. Immediately they began to pressure her. "You must let him move back in," the elders told her. "Divorce is always wrong."

Linda, the wife, was gracious in response. "I don't think you know what's really going on. I have sought the Lord about this and shared it with some other believers closest to me. They believe I'm doing the right thing."

One elder, Jeff, began to argue with Linda, invoking God's judgment if she did not obey. I stopped him in mid-tirade and turned to her and said, "Linda, you know that no one has the right to demand that you deny your conscience. I know you love the Lord and are trying to follow him. If what Jeff has said is God's heart for you, I have no doubt God will show you. If not, feel free to toss it." I prayed for God to lead her with his wisdom and courage despite what others thought, and we excused ourselves.

Outside Jeff tore into me, telling me that I had defied God's will. I told him that I disagreed, that she obviously was walking this out with other believers, and that it was not his place to demand her obedience. Months later we found out what she had chosen not to tell us that evening. Her husband had made some sexual overtures to her children from a previous marriage and had persistently refused her offer to get counseling. She had separated to protect them.

## Letting People Have Their Journey

If anyone had the right to command obedience, it would have been Jesus when he lived in the flesh. That, however, is not how he treated people. He presented truth to them and in doing so gave them a simple option: They could follow his way or not. He let people have their journey because he wanted them to follow out of the conviction of their conscience and not because he could threaten or cajole them into conformity. He modeled God's love to everyone, knowing the joy of participating in the Father's family was far more effective than strict obedience.

Paul demonstrated the same wisdom and compassion as he spread the gospel. He renounced secret and shameful ways of manipulating people into God's life. Instead, he said, "By setting forth the truth plainly we commend ourselves to every man's conscience in the sight of God" (2 Cor. 4:2). He knew that the power of the gospel did not lie in making people act Christian, but in putting them in touch with the mystery of the gospel—Christ in them, the hope of glory (Col. 1:27). In other words, we help others be transformed not by getting them to conform to our rules but by encouraging their dependence on Jesus. The difference is remarkable. Those who know the Father and understand the way he works will never demand your submission. In fact, they know that doing so will subvert his working.

Paul made his case most graphically to the Colossians. In 2:16–19 he told them not to let *anyone* judge them regarding what they ate or what celebrations they attended. He reminded them that those who try to command others prove by doing so that they have "lost connection with the

Head, from whom the whole body, supported and held together by its ligaments and sinews, grows as God causes it to grow" (v. 19).

Paul knew that only Jesus changes lives. People who lose sight of that truth end up telling others how to live—a fruitless and abusive endeavor. Even the apostle Paul didn't demand that others do what he thought best. In 1 Corinthians 16:12 Paul "strongly urged" Apollos to go with some other believers but noted that he was unwilling. Paul obviously didn't agree with Apollos, but he didn't condemn his choice or break fellowship with him. He concluded by saying that "he will go when he has the opportunity." Submission allows us to offer input and receive it from others while still recognizing that they and we are free to use it as Jesus leads us.

By letting others have their journey and not forcing them onto ours, we can be honest about where we see things differently, and we can continue to love them even when they don't do what we think is right. By freeing others from our judgment, our friendships can continue to grow instead of being snatched away from us by disagreements. Remember, God will work with others, even using what we consider to be mistakes to draw them deeper into his life and make them more sensitive to his voice.

## When in Rome

I hate squash. I hate everything about squash. As a guest in someone's home, however, my dislikes are not important. Once I sat down at a table where our plates had already been filled. On mine sat a heaping helping of cooked squash. As we started to eat, I looked at the two young children eating with us. "Do we all clean our plates in this house?" I asked them.

"We certainly do," the mother replied with a wink. Without another word I ate the squash—all of it. That is what you do when you are in someone else's house. (Of course, if you are allergic to squash and it would make you swell up and die, I think you could let others know that.)

Our freedom in Christ allows us to go into any situation with the ability to get along with others while still living authentically. When I go into someone's home or meet with a group of believers, I am very aware that I'm a guest. Thus, I sometimes sing songs I don't like and listen politely even when people are wandering into left field. But if we have the opportunity for dialogue, I certainly contribute my thoughts. While I may offer people a chance to think outside the box, I won't act as a change agent—unless they ask, of course!

Submission means I will go along with what others have agreed to do as long as I do not have to violate my conscience. For the most part, I go along, honestly contributing where appropriate. In the rare instance that I cannot go along, I will honestly tell why I can't and excuse myself. That too is submission.

## Patience with Everyone

The further you are along in this journey, the easier it will be for you to get along with others, even those who are weaker in the faith. Romans 14 and 1 Corinthians 8 used to plague me. These passages clearly ask those who are stronger in the faith to yield to those who are weaker. That sounds like a recipe for disaster. How can we yield to the conscience of the weak without letting them lead others astray?

Paul builds his case for submission on the fact that Jesus is the head of the church and before him each of us will stand or fall. As brothers and sisters we don't tell one another what to do but maintain an honest dialogue that respects God's working in our lives. We are to follow Jesus, not intermediaries who tell us what God wants.

Have you ever noticed that the early apostles never asked anyone to violate their conscience? They never saw themselves above others in the body of Christ but alongside them to share the journey. Even when the Corinthians sought Paul's thoughts on whether meat that had been sacrificed to idols and then sold at the local butcher shop was thus tainted with evil and therefore harmful for believers, he did not ask anyone to override his or her conscience in that matter. He told them the truth about their situation. Idols are nothing; therefore meat offered to them was nothing, and believers were free to eat it. But then he added that if their consciences were not free to eat it because they thought it was spiritually tainted, they shouldn't eat it (1 Cor. 8:1–13).

Paul said there is an objective truth here, but if your conscience doesn't know it, you are better off to follow your conscience. Why? Because Paul knew that is how God leads his people. Never talk others out of following their consciences. Even if they are wrong, letting them follow it is the fastest way to God changing it. Paul even added that if he were going to eat with people whose consciences were offended by meat offered to idols, he wouldn't eat it either. It is not worth destroying the kingdom of God over something as mundane as food. That's freedom! You are not free to do something unless you are also free not to!

Paul understood submission not as something he demanded of others, but as that which freed him to serve others. Always be careful when following God's leading comes at someone else's expense. When God puts something on your heart, you will find that he will ask you to take the risk and not put it on others.

As Richard Foster said in *Celebration of Discipline,* submission "is the ability to lay down the terrible burden of always needing to get your own way."[4] Can you imagine what it would be like to live in the freedom of God working out his life in you without having to scheme to make things turn out the way you want? As you learn the joy of submission, you will find selfishness and independence as abhorrent as I do cooked squash.

## Sharing Input with One Another

When we lose the notion that submission is a tool to control one another, we can feast on its fruits by sharing our wisdom and insight. I rarely teach publicly something new that I haven't shared with half a dozen others in personal conversation, seeking their input and counsel. I don't always take their advice, but I do listen and make room for what others are saying—especially those I know to be further along the journey than I am.

I have one friend who submits anything he senses God leading him to do to the believer near him who is not the most likely to agree with him. He is looking for God's wisdom, not a rubber stamp. He knows that if someone who approaches life differently comes to the same conclusion he did, he will have more confidence in God's leading. Of course this does not work with those who have a vested interest in the outcome of your actions. Be careful that their counsel is not tainted by their own agenda.

God enjoys confirming his work by two or three voices so we can walk with confidence. When he is teaching me something, I'll often see it in the Scriptures, read about it in another book, and hear someone bring it up in conversation. Submitting our thoughts and insights to others allows us to expand our seeing and hearing by including the eyes and ears of other believers around us. Our own perspectives can be limited and distorted by blind spots. The different vantage points that people have on my life or my actions often help me distinguish between God's leading and my own desires.

I got up early one morning inspired to write a letter to a group of believers who had been maliciously spreading lies about me. I was so excited by how articulately I had exposed their sin and by how humble and gracious I looked that I called a good friend to read it to him.

When I finished he said, "That's a great letter—your best yet! But now you need to throw it away without mailing it." I couldn't believe my ears. Throw it away? I was sure he would be as excited as I was. I began to argue with him and offered a list of reasons why he was wrong. When I paused to let him agree with me, he said gently, "I thought you told me you were going to trust God with your reputation. It doesn't sound like that letter does that."

I told my friend that I had trusted God with my reputation for two years, and now it was time for truth. I was determined to ignore his advice and mail the letter anyway, but over the next few hours his words began to sink in. In the end, I didn't mail it; and by hindsight I know that was the right thing to do. I realized that my friends wouldn't need a defense, and those I thought needed it wouldn't believe it. I left my reputation in God's hands, and through that painful experience I learned why Paul said trying to please people and living in service to God are two different paths. Without my friend's willingness to speak up, not only would I have caused greater pain for others, but I also would have missed out on discovering freedom from the tyranny of other people's opinions.

None of us has been asked to make our journey alone. A wealth of knowledge and insight awaits you in the lives of believers all around you. The beauty of a relationship that shares the journey at this level is difficult to describe. While it may be rare in our day, by partnering with others through submission, we can experience the deepest joy human relationships have to offer.

## Discussion Questions

1. Can you think of a time someone demanded that you submit to him or her when you didn't feel right about doing so? Did it help? How did it make you feel?
2. Tell about a time when someone's insight changed the course of your life.
3. Why will submission never ask you to go against your conscience?
4. How can you share together more effectively the insights and wisdom God has given to others?

# 13

# treasures waiting to be discovered

> We are not our problems. We are not our wounds. We are not our sins. We are persons of radical worth and unrevealed beauty.
>
> Larry Crabb

Darrell worked at the city golf course where I played. Though we had exchanged greetings on a first-name basis many times, I had no idea of the depth of God's working in his life—that was, until my son took some golf lessons from him.

Darrell had insisted that I join them for the lesson, and he worked on my game as well. One of the things he said over and over again was, "You've got to let the golf club work your hands instead of your hands working the golf club."

On one occasion, hoping to open a door into a deeper conversation with him, I answered, "You sound like my friend in Australia."

"Really, what does he say about your swing?"

"He's not a golfer. His comments were about my life, not my swing. He said I needed to learn to let God control my life instead of trying to control God."

"He's exactly right," Darrell said with a twinkle in his eye. After the lesson we both pursued the conversation and discovered that we shared a common passion for the reality of God's presence and that we had learned many of the same lessons in the last few years. Not long after that we went to lunch, and in the seven years since then, we have forged a depth of friendship and fellowship that has encouraged both of us through difficult as well as joyous times.

You never know what treasure of God's glory might sit across from you on the bus, down the hall at work, or even in the house next door. The only way to find out is to engage every person you meet with love, gentleness, and respect; and throughout your journey you will find that God has scattered a vast array of people around your path who hold a wealth of insight and encouragement to help you.

I hope by now that you have already thought about how you will treat the next person who crosses your path. Whether it is a believer in need of fellowship or an unbeliever in need of exposure to the love of our wonderful Savior, just ask Jesus to make you sensitive to the people who literally pass you every day. Of course you will not touch them all, but there may be a handful every day whom you can touch with a simple expression of the Father's love.

If you have read this far alone, perhaps now is the time to consider a journey of greater depth—exploring what it means to walk together with other believers and learning how to share God's life together. Jesus didn't come to found a religion; he came to rebuild his Father's family. He wants to link you with other believers in authentic relationships that allow you to recover the lost art of one anothering, and the joy of those friendships can be just around the corner.

I know that can be scary, especially if you have been deeply hurt by other believers. But it is worth tearing down your defense mechanisms and once again learning what it means to love people freely and to share the journey with those who also desire to be transformed by God.

Yes, you will still meet some people who allow their bondages to bleed all over you, but you will find the freedom to walk away guiltlessly from any attempts to manipulate you. As you learn to love as you are loved, you will find yourself free to tell people no whenever they push you to do what isn't in your heart to do. Loving them does not mean you have to submit to their control. Just let them know that you care about them, but that the relationship isn't working for you. They may try to pin you down to an explanation, but you don't owe them one. Life is too short and good relationships are too awesome to waste time trying to fix destructive ones.

You will meet even more people who are just like you, pilgrims on a journey to know Jesus better. Though one anothering can only begin with what you are willing to give away, you will find God providing others who will help you. What persons do you feel drawn to, or what friendships would you like to see become even more fruitful? Could that nudging be the Holy Spirit?

Invite some people out to lunch or over for an evening together. It doesn't have to be fancy. As you get to know them better, tell them of your hunger to experience real Christian community and see if they are interested. Suggest getting together regularly and learning how to live out the joy of one anothering. You may even consider reading and discussing this book together. You will find that many people around you are a vast treasure waiting to be discovered. Their stories will encourage you, their insights will free you, and their help will lighten your journey.

Until ten years ago, many of my friendships with fellow travelers on the Christian journey were laced with trip wires that would bring anger and resentment without warning. It was amazing to see how fast I could go from beloved brother to dangerous outcast whenever I failed to meet someone's expectations or demands on my life. (To be honest, I did some of that manipulating myself.)

For the last decade, however, I have been able to share relationships in God's family that I have always dreamed of having. I have found those friendships right in my hometown, in a new community my family moved to a few years ago, and all over the world. Most of the time when I'm getting off an airplane somewhere in the world, I'm met by people I have known only through email or phone calls. Sometimes within a few minutes we are sharing some of the deepest struggles of the journey and finding great encouragement in doing so.

This is the kind of community God created us to experience. It may start with just two or three. You may have a false start or two as some who seem interested suddenly cool. Don't take their lack of interest personally and retreat behind the wall of your defenses. God has a lot of other people who will be helped by the treasure he has put in you. Keep asking him, and keep your eyes peeled for relationships that God brings into your life.

Innumerable human treasures are waiting to be opened, and many of them feel adrift in the superficial relationships they already have. I am amazed at the great number of people in the world who have a genuine hunger for God and are thirsting for Jesus-centered friendships that offer mutual support and care. Living out those friendships is one of the greatest gifts of being in the Father's family. It is the difference between "going to church" and "being the church" at every moment wherever you are in the world.

# Appendix

## sharing the journey with others

This book can be used as a thirteen-week guide through the one anothering passages of the New Testament to help you cultivate rich relationships with other believers. The discussion questions at the end of each chapter are designed to help a group of people build life-changing, Jesus-centered friendships. You may already be meeting with a small group, or you may want to invite a few friends to study the book together. Your group may be as small as two or three or as large as fifteen. A group any larger than that, however, will tend to make the study more of an intellectual exercise than a relational experience.

Here are two tips for making your time more effective. First, don't ever think a book like this of itself can engender the relationships that make body life possible. Only Jesus by the power of the Holy Spirit can knit his body together, opening our eyes to what real love is and equipping us to share that love with others. Make sure this does not become a mere human exercise. Ask him to lead you in it and beyond it, creating among you relationships as only he can.

Second, if you are not meeting with a group of people who normally gather, you may want to work through a few housekeeping details first. The goal is for your group to have a wide-ranging conversation about members' growth in Jesus and their desire to share his life effectively with other believers. If that happens in the freedom of just being brothers and sisters together, then feel free to skip this section. If, however, you feel that some guidelines may be helpful as you start out, read over the list below and sort out some of the details that will help your group function effectively. This doesn't have to take a long time. Simply find a consensus on each and move to the next.

## Housekeeping Details

1. Do we want to set a regular time to get together each week? Each month?
2. Do we want to start with a simple meal or plan refreshments together during or after?
3. If we don't know one another well, do we want to plan a special night together when each will share ten minutes on his or her spiritual journey up to this point? (Or, as an alternative, you may agree to get together in groups of three or four for a meal in the first couple of weeks to do the same thing.)
4. Do we want to have someone facilitate our dialogue together? (It may be best to rotate that role among those who are willing to serve in that capacity instead of having the same person do it all the time.)

5. Do we want to have a brief time of praise and prayer together before we begin?
6. Do we want a definite finish time for our meeting so we can make arrangements accordingly?

## Recommendations for Effective Discussion

1. Encourage a safe environment in which any question or comment can be made without people feeling stupid or put-down.
2. Make sure that no one is forced to share if he or she doesn't want to, but that everyone has an opportunity to add insights. (Those who find it easier to speak in group settings may hold back a bit to make room for others, and those who feel as if their input is unimportant might take some risks to add their insights to the others.)
3. Don't let anyone take the role of an expert, but facilitate an environment of joint discovery about the things God wants to do in all of your lives through this study.
4. Have the freedom to disagree at times without having to convince others that you are right or damage the relationship of caring and concern for one another.

# notes

1. http://www.brainyquote.com/quotes/quotes/e/q105229.html
2. NASA curriculum posted at: http://nasaexplores.com/lessons/ 01–071 /5–8_2.html
3. John W. Yates, "Pottering and Prayer," *Christianity Today,* April 2, 2001.
4. Richard Foster, *Celebration of Discipline* (New York: Harper and Row, 1988), 97.

**Wayne Jacobsen** lives in Oxnard, California, but travels internationally as director of Lifestream Ministries (http://www.lifestream.org). He is a contributing editor to Leadership Journal and the author of *The Naked Church, In My Father's Vineyard,* and *He Loved Me.*

**Clay Jacobsen,** Wayne's brother, has directed the Jerry Lewis Telethon, *Dr. Laura, Entertainment Tonight,* and *Prime Time Country.* He is the author of *The Lasko Interview* and *Circle of Seven* and resides in Camarillo, California. See http://www.clayjacobsen.com.